# Now You Sue Them, Now You Don't

# Now You Sue Them, Now You Don't

## The Magic of Mediating

Vincent P. Fornias

Copyright © 2021 Full Court Press, an imprint of Fastcase, Inc.

All rights reserved.

No part of this book may be reproduced in any form—by microfilm, xerography, or otherwise—or incorporated into any information retrieval system without the written permission of the copyright owner. For customer support, please contact Fastcase, Inc., 711 D St. NW, Suite 200, Washington, D.C. 20004, 202.999.4777 (phone), 202.521.3462 (fax), or email customer service at support@fastcase.com.

A Full Court Press, Fastcase, Inc., Publication.

Printed and bound in the United States of America.

10 9 8 7 6 5 4 3 2 1

ISBN (print): 978-1-949884-46-3
ISBN (online): 978-1-949884-47-0

The cover of this book features ilbusca/DigitalVision Vectors via Getty Images

*To my father, Vicente J. Fornias,
for his unwavering work ethic, and
my mother, Marta Polo Fornias,
whose optimistic soul and ribald sense of the
absurd were unmatched.*

An aging Irish priest addicted to the game of golf found himself on the 18th hole facing a daunting 200-yard approach shot over water to a narrow green. He bravely pulled his seldom used one-iron from his bag. In the middle of his downswing the heavens opened with a blinding flash of lightning and a deafening roll of thunder, splitting in half a nearby tree. The spectacle caused him to badly top his shot into the water. This produced a heretical display by the man of the cloth, ranting loudly and cursing God as he threateningly waved his club to the clouds above. His caddy, greatly alarmed, ran up to him, and yanking the club from his grasp, admonished him, "Father, have ye gone mad? You can't wave a club around like that in the middle of a thunderstorm!" The priest turned to him and mockingly declared, "Pfft. Not even God can hit a one-iron!"

—Old golf war story

# Contents

Foreword ...................................................................... xi
Introduction .................................................................xiii

Chapter 1. Hitting the Beachhead ................................. 1
Chapter 2. The Arrows in Your Quiver ........................... 5
Chapter 3. Weapons of Mass Distraction ...................... 17
Chapter 4. Prepping the Roux ....................................... 23
Chapter 5. We Are All Gathered Here Today ................. 31
Chapter 6. The Early Caucuses: "I *Think* I Can ..." ....... 39
Chapter 7. Late Caucuses: "I *Know* I Can ..." ............... 47
Chapter 8. The Marlin Is Next to the Boat:
  Grab the Net! ............................................................ 59
Chapter 9. Truth or Consequences .............................. 63
Chapter 10. Taking Care of Business ........................... 69
Chapter 11. Are We Having Fun Yet? ........................... 75
Chapter 12. Razzle-Dazzle ........................................... 79

Epilogue. Closing Thoughts: Into the Mystic ................ 83

# Foreword

Vince and I both grew up in New Orleans. We did not know each other until much later when we crossed paths as lawyers. We immediately found a close friendship, not just because we were both New Orleanians, but primarily because we went to rival high schools and engage in a constant banter about whose high school afforded us a better education. In New Orleans it is more important where you went to high school than where you went to college. Mine, of course, was superior, and he will have to admit that ... someday.

I have known Vince for all of our 40+ years of law practice, first as a noble adversary, and then, for the past 30 years or so until his retirement, as the best mediator in Louisiana, if not the South. If you had a tough case, with bad facts (on either side), multiple parties, intractable liens, and hard-to-deal-with clients, Vince was your go-to mediator. If it was an impossible case, you needed Vince Fornias to mediate it.

Vince was a natural problem solver, bringing to the table a lifetime of trying and mediating thousands of difficult cases, unsurpassed preparation, and an unrivaled sense of humor. These assets are essential to success in resolving disputes, especially the humor, which lightens an often lethal mood.

This book is a fascinating compendium of advice, war stories, and poignant reminisces about how to get to a resolution in difficult controversies with difficult people. It should be required reading for mediators, would-be mediators, judges who try to settle cases, and lawyers who mediate difficult matters.

... and it is funny.

Edward J. Walters, Jr.<br>
August 2020

# Introduction

A while back I received a mediation position paper from an experienced trial lawyer, a veteran of many courtroom settings and scores of mediations. Right smack in the middle of his submission, he made the following observation:

> Plaintiff has no real loss of wages. She works in an enjoyable job. Obviously she is not an attorney. Maybe she's a mediator.

It is a fact of legal life that the vast majority of litigators—and almost all trial judges—are convinced that their easy fallback position is to be a mediator. Not so subtly, they express the attitude that mediators have hit the career jackpot as under-challenged, overpaid message carriers. Perhaps this view is a symptom of feeling burned out or unappreciated in their own career choices. There is the fable of The Messiah making his long-awaited return. He notices a blind man, comforts him, and restores his vision, advising him to go in peace. Then he encounters a crippled woman, and listening to her tale of woe, miraculously cures her affliction, with the words to "go in peace." Finally, he encounters a trial lawyer with a couple of decades of experience. He sits next to him—and both weep.

I could have been that third person many years ago. By then, I had tried my share of cases and was becoming tired and cynical of our litigation system. One day I was summoned to a meeting among trial counsel in a products liability case in the Lafayette, Louisiana, office of the plaintiff's lawyer. When I arrived, we were all introduced to this man from Texas who called himself a professional mediator. He requested that each of us contact our respective clients—the plaintiff was already in attendance—and we proceeded to meet in a conference room and air our respective positions. He allowed the plaintiff to speak his piece with our clients on speaker phones. Then he engaged in private and confidential shuttle diplomacy with each of the lawyers and their clients. I was attending my first mediation—by accident. The matter did not settle that day, but it did so with some follow-up calls by that mediator within a matter of days. We were all impressed.

As mediations became more and more popular in the areas of personal injury and others, I attended hundreds of them advocating for my clients, both defendants and plaintiffs. Over the next few years I was exposed to a wide variety of advocacy styles and more importantly to dramatically contrasting methods used by presiding mediators. Like most other litigators, I had my short list of those with whom I felt most comfortable, because I could trust them to work hard to help settle my cases. I even wrote a cynical humor piece in a legal publication in which I described "The Rules" for surviving a typical mediation:

### The Rules

1. Pre-mediation nutrition is essential. Serious carbo-packing should commence at least 48 hours prior to the opening session. Unless you're partial to the likes of Purina Po-Boys, you will engage enthusiastically in the traditional practice of Pre-Mediation Stuffing (PMS), involving shoving

Snickers, King Dons, trail mix, and anything else you can stuff into your suit pockets, much like a ground squirrel engorging its cheeks prior to a frigid day's activities. Post-Halloween mediations are particularly successful.

2. Appropriate attire is *de rigueur*. Plaintiffs themselves should be garbed in dark-pigmented mournful fabric, preferably without turquoise studs or leather. Their counsel should wear subdued tones and ditch their sneakers. Defense lawyers and their clients should dust off their car-buying ensembles, appearing as shallow-pocketed as Hank Fonda in "The Grapes of Wrath."

3. Unless you're a certified computer nerd and are able to do more with your notebook than figure out how to open it, you will need suitable fare to while away the eons between productive discussions. Some prefer reading material ranging from *War and Peace* to Shelby Foote's *The Civil War: A Narrative* (in three volumes). Others may use the opportunity to Berlitz their way to a new language, say, Mandarin Chinese.

4. Avoid personal hygiene for at least 24 hours prior to the start. If you're one of those health nuts, then at least partake of lots of Greek food, or splash on a gallon or two of Schwegmann's bay rum. No holds are barred in the unceasing efforts to avoid that dreadful closed-door Dutch Uncle session, known as a "caucus" [Arabic, *cau*-(drop) *cus* (pants)].

5. The opening statement is your best chance to create the appropriate atmosphere for fruitful movement. If you would like the day to go somewhat faster, use carefully measured power words

such as "absolutely," "inconceivable," "weasel," or "Bogalusa," or phrases such as "Ready, boots? Start walkin'."

6. As noted above, private caucus invitations are like being sent to the principal's office. If you feel the mediator's icy tentacles on your shoulder, immediately claim mistaken identity. See Rule 2 above regarding mediation attire. Elvis, Jimmy Hoffa, and Princess Anastasia have been known to thrive in certain mediations.

7. If, despite your best effort, you find yourself behind closed doors with a mediator staring directly at your wallet, respond to his inevitable "dream scenario" suggestion with an effective gesture of detached incredulity. Eye-rolling is for the hopelessly uninitiated. Contemptuous snorts followed by a strongly uttered, "Excuse me, but are you on some sort of medication?" are somewhat more effective.

8. A corollary to Rule 7. At all costs, take no notes during a caucus, or risk being instantly branded as Someone Who Cares.

9. As in other competitive sports, Image Is Everything during this process. If you are interested in retaining your client, do not mingle with the opposition within 100 feet of a mediation site. Instead, the enemy should be looked upon as Hirohito at Pearl Harbor or Santa Ana at The Alamo. Collegiality ain't kosher when your client's entire world view is on the line.

10. If by chance you reach some sort of accord despite your client, strive for tasteful closure of the session. This excludes high fives and "We're Not Worthy" gestures, or animated utterances of

"Cha-Ching" and "Nah Nah Nah Nah, Hey Hey, Good-Bye."

Then, one defining day, I was contacted by a client whom I had represented in many prior mediations. He made a strange and intimidating request. He informed me that the mediator on an upcoming matter had canceled out with a family emergency and asked if, after disclosing my prior representation on other cases to all parties, I was interested in being the mediator in the case. I don't know whether it was naiveté, arrogance, insanity, or curiosity that caused me to accept the challenge. Providentially, all the parties agreed to give me a shot. That case didn't settle—but I was hooked.

Soon I was signing up for formal mediation training and reading a lot about mediation and negotiation as time permitted in my litigation practice. I then took the next scary step, putting out "the word" among my litigation cohorts that I was interested in being considered for their mediations. I was honored to be given that opportunity by some, then by others. And now, almost before I knew it, almost 4,000 mediations later, I have passed the torch to others.

In tribute to the timeless lyrics sung by Joe South to "walk a mile in my shoes," I humbly share with you my stories and thoughts on becoming a successful mediator.

# Now You Sue Them, Now You Don't

# Chapter 1

# Hitting the Beachhead

Time for your first reality check? Unfortunately, many in our profession have as much chance of mediating for a living as my rescue dogs have of winning Westminster. In a subsequent chapter, you will read about certain personality traits that are crucial to succeed in the world of mediations. Without them, you face a steep uphill climb. In addition to these, your professional reputation precedes you. If right or wrong, you are regarded as untrustworthy, unfair, lazy, or all of the above, then save yourself the trouble of reading further.

Similar sobering news goes to those fresh out of law school. I have often been asked as a guest speaker at law school classes how one goes about becoming a mediator. My answer, much like the musician who yearns to get to Carnegie Hall, is to "practice, practice, then practice some more." Basically, without the battle scars that definitively show that you've "been there, done that, got that holey T-shirt," your credibility will be sorely challenged. I once analogized a mediator's required practical background to the following recipe from my own experience:

> Start with a couple of decades in courthouse trenches; bring to a boil with multiple appearances

at state and federal courts of appeal and the Louisiana Supreme Court; simmer with a graveyard of dashed hopes in most of these settings; and season to taste with service as an advocate in hundreds of mediations.

Having made this point, I do not mean to imply that experience alone will help you succeed as a mediator. There is indeed a method to the science and the art of negotiating and mediating, and that requires synthesizing your practical experience with some formal training to understand the dynamics of your task. Among many educational options (ranging from a few days to a full semester), prominently included in no particular order are Strauss Institute for Dispute Resolution at Pepperdine University School of Law; Harvard University Negotiation Project; Northwestern University; and The Association of Attorney-Mediators, based in Dallas. Additionally, private mediation firms offer their own in-house training for prospective members of their respective neutral panels.

Once these steps are taken, it's time to pound the proverbial pavement to make a niche for yourself in Mediationland. Far too many would-be mediators envision this as the simple exercise by Lucy in the *Peanuts* cartoon of hanging out a shingle proclaiming that "The [Mediator] Is In." Good luck with that. In truth, there is no such shortcut to starting and building a mediation practice. There is no substitute for personal solicitations of business from fellow attorneys (both prior allies and past opponents), members of the judiciary, and even past and present clients. These contacts can take the form of visits, personal notes, or letters, or emails. As stated before, your hope is that these gestures will be well received by a significant number of associates in the legal world who consider you able, trustworthy, hardworking, and fair. You should also explore qualifying for bar registries that contain lists of eligible mediators in a particular district (See, for example, La. Mediation Act, La. R.S. 9:4101, et seq.). You should make yourself available to speak on the topic of mediations or negotiations for the various bar association groups as well as prominent industry groups. Do not overlook speaking in law school settings, as this is your chance to make a first impression on those about to enter the profession who may soon be looking for a mediator.

Once the door is opened, do not let it slam behind you. If you receive an assignment, prepare, work hard, do it well and with full commitment. One of my early mediations in a complicated patent infringement case went until 2:30 in the morning before the matter (thankfully) settled. I received many future referrals from those participants, who saw that as a mediator, I was "all in" with them for the duration. Good news indeed does travel at warp speed! If the matter settles, it is a good practice to follow up with a personal note thanking the lawyers for their commitment to the process. *Do not* take credit for the settlement (I often tell parties I neither take credit for a settlement nor for a failed mediation), but express your appreciation for their hard work in the process and for giving you the opportunity to be of some assistance in their efforts.

Indeed, even if a matter does not settle at mediation, let the dust settle a few days and then routinely follow up to make absolutely certain there is no more movement that is possible. If you are told by one party that there is no further need for follow-ups, inform the other parties that it is not you who is giving up. Most parties will appreciate your continuing efforts, and will take note of it in future decisions on choosing a mediator.

Chapter 2

# The Arrows in Your Quiver

*This above all—to thine own self be true,
And it must follow, as the night the day,
Thou can'st not then
Be false to any man.*

—Hamlet, Act I, Scene 3

The discussion to follow describes the ideal intellectual and personality traits of a successful mediator. To some extent, you can develop them, but there are some that either are or are not part of your genetic makeup. The worst thing you can do is try to hide being yourself (as seedy and detestable as you might be!). With that in mind, here is my short list of desirable traits.

## The Ability to Tactfully Undermine False Perceptions About Mediators or the Process

You do this mainly by showing yourself to be a determined, committed, and competitive professional. Here is a graphic example. I was once one of several lawyers involved in a multiparty mediation conducted by a Houston-based mediator. He charged a $10,000.00 minimum advance fee, and billed hourly portal-to-portal, plus expenses. We had a traditional opening session, then he conducted all of two caucuses. Total time elapsed was less than two hours. He then gathered everyone back together, and looking somewhat downcast, declared that we were much too far apart, and that it would be a waste of our time to continue. One of my more outspoken cohorts looked at him incredulously and replied, "Listen, pal, we've already paid you $10K to do your job. We got you reserved for the day. If you think you're goin' home now, you're sadly mistaken. If you can't be of any use as a mediator, then I'm takin' you home with me and you can mow my lawn and wash my car. You still wanna give up so easy?" Surprised and somewhat intimidated, the mediator had a private meeting with that lawyer, then resumed the mediation, and the dispute settled late that afternoon. No bucket, sponges, or lawn mowers were necessary.

I have witnessed some mediators act like mere carrier pigeons, going back and forth down the hall, sticking their heads into one caucus room or another (not even closing the door behind them!), announcing the other room's latest offer, and simply asking for their counteroffer. I suggest to you that if you are just going through the motions, you do both yourself and the profession a terrible disservice. You are hired to be proactive and energetic in helping the parties come together. As it is, too many lawyers have the attitude expressed to me by a litigator who bragged that his goal was to wait until every lawyer except him became a mediator, so he could have all the litigation work to himself. If the legal profession thinks we are a fungible and inconsequential commodity, we are all in trouble. Instead, adopt the spirit of the legendary football coach Paul "Bear" Bryant, who was reputed to have told an opposing coach, "You may beat me, but bring a sack lunch and a big stick, because it'll take you a while."

## Your Powers as a Poker Player

Some people have incredibly broad intuitive abilities. Others are accountants. As a mediator, the right, or intuitive, side of your brain is far more important to your functioning. Do not get me wrong. That left side cannot be ignored as you collect and process information and data crucial to your understanding of the case. But what you do with that information and when and how you do it is far more important.

One experienced negotiator has described this quality as "listening with three ears." One ear hears what is actually being said, the other ear perceives what is being meant "between the lines" of what is said, and a third ear focuses on the message sent by what has *not* been said.

The indirect communication by parties to a mediation can often make or break a mediation. One study, published by psychological researcher Dr. Albert Mehrabian in 1967, found that humans communicate in face-to-face meetings as follows:

Body language: 55%
Tone of voice: 38%
Actual words spoken: 7%

Body language can take many forms. One party may be expressing an opinion or listening to a varying position while subconsciously "steepling," a process implying superiority in the manner his two thumbs support his face while other opposing fingers touch at the tips in front of the face in the rough form of a church steeple. Other telltale body signs include leg folding or arms crossed, which often express resistance or defensiveness to someone else's position. The opposite emotional reaction is displayed by someone who leans forward when hearing a position. Some people play poker better than others. Heavy eye-blinking or blushing often denotes insincerity or a feeling of discomfort.

## The Ability to Listen Intently and Over a *Long* Period of Time

A close relative to right-brain perceptions is the power to really concentrate on what someone is saying. You will notice that I will refer repeatedly in this work to the great Hall of Famer of the New York Yankees, the inimitable master of malapropisms, Yogi Berra. If he were quoted correctly, I suspect that Yogi might have made a formidable mediator. One pronouncement he once made was that "you can observe a lot by watching." Think about that. Too many mediators, instead of leaning forward and processing what is before them, engage in accidental or intentional one-upmanship with a party. This often takes the form of endless personal war stories or exhibiting a "you think that's bad?" tone that implies he can't wait until the other party finishes talking so that he can wow him with his own more important views. Others are as stiff as an old man on a winter morning.

A nationally renowned mediator, Jeff Krivis, has written about the science of listening to enable a mediator to engage in four invaluable mediation objectives, which he summarizes in the acronym of VECS. Listening allows you to "Validate," or acknowledge what a party is saying; to "Empathize" with his perspective; to "Clarify" what the person is saying, to be sure we are on the same page of understanding; and finally to "Summarize" that understanding, which can be used later in a mediation to remind a party of his prior commitment to a needed position.

A by-product of faulty listening is the inability to register and act upon what I refer to as "waffly" words being spoken, words that will give you an insight into the party's real position or show a potential malleability. Great examples of this phenomenon can be found in almost any episode of the popular reality series *Pawn Stars*, featuring the interaction of the owners of a Las Vegas pawn shop with prospective customers. The series is a tutorial on active listening and reading between the lines. Often a seller will be asked what he wants for his treasured item, and he will reply with, "Well, I'd like to get $____." The "like" word is akin to blood in front of a great white shark, prompting the owner to acridly reply with a sarcastic comment like, "Well, I'd like to spend a night with Charlize Theron, but that ain't gonna happen either." At this point, the poor seller is in a position similar to a lonely trembling field mouse scurrying vainly away from the pouncing talons of a voracious hawk.

Other "waffly" words include "about," or "thereabouts," or "want." The latter word is an open invitation to quote in reply Mick Jagger's classic lyrics that "you can't always get what you want, but if you try sometime, you get what you need." Another baseball Hall of Famer, the great base stealer Rickey Henderson, once tried to justify his holdout for a better contract by declaring, "All Ricky needs is what Ricky wants." Perhaps if he had reversed the phrases he may have been more successful!

Let me share one personal example of how active listening ultimately made the difference at the end of a mediation day. The matter involved a personal injury claim where plaintiff was represented by an "unconventional" lawyer who loved to dress flamboyantly and informally, almost as an "in your face" statement to the silk stocking defense lawyer crowd. On this day, he donned a silk short-sleeve shirt with an elaborately colored Oriental motif. The insurance adjuster, a conservative grizzled vet of decades in the industry, had a hard time accepting his attire, and it became obvious that this was interfering with his commitment to negotiating in good faith.

Despite my tactful advice not to underestimate plaintiff's counsel despite his wardrobe choice, the adjuster persisted with an almost punitive negotiation style that was anathema to the mind-set of his impatient and short-tempered opponent. Finally we were within shouting range of each room's walkaway figure, with everyone drawing a line in the sand on further movement. Serendipitously, the adjuster had made during the day several similar pejorative comments under his breath about his opponent's colorful outfit. That opened the door for a proposed face-saver, wherein the adjuster was persuaded to add a small difference-making amount to his written final settlement sum—with the proviso that this was not only in exchange for a final dismissal of the suit, but also "for one silk shirt with matching cobras in front." Holding my breath, I brought the written proposal into plaintiff counsel's room and asked that he consider it, emphasizing that he had obviously made the adjuster blink with the uptick in the defense's offer and suggesting that he had succeeded in getting under the adjuster's skin, producing the obviously face-saving wardrobe demand. Without saying a word, he took the written proposal, opened the door, marched to the defense room, yanked the door open (scatter!)—and silently undid the top two buttons of his shirt. He then dramatically pulled it off pullover style, laid it on the table, and exclaimed, "Show me da money!" The sight of his hairy torso alone prompted defendants to throw in court costs and mediation fees, just to flee the scene.

## A Sense of Timing

This is another trait that activates the right side of your brain. It is a fact that each mediation has countless crossroads and forks in the road. Some are dead ends. Yogi would describe this sixth sense as, "When you come to a fork in the road, take it." In any given mediation, a mediator will need to play radically different roles to keep the parties on the road to consensus. There is no one roadmap that reaches the promised land.

In general, the early caucuses call more on your abilities in disarming lack of trust in you or the process and building rapport through compassion and proof of your understanding of each party's position. Recall the "VECS" acronym referred to earlier. I am old enough to recall when Al Franken was a TV comedy star on *Saturday Night Live* long before he commenced his political career. My favorite Franken role was the gentle, alpaca sweater–wearing life coach named Stuart Smalley. Through his over-the-top affirmative style, Smalley enabled his clientele to reach the three V's often required in the early caucuses—Validation, Vindication, and Venting. In these nascent stages in the plaintiffs' room, I will genuinely affirm to them my acknowledgment that there is no doubt in my mind that, rather than accepting any amount of money for their damages, they would trade it for a time machine or magic wand that would place them elsewhere instead of where the accident befell them and changed their lives. At this point, hopefully they will share with me their story and show appreciation for my empathy with their trust.

Parties are not the only ones that often need validation in these early stages. Lawyers have egos (imagine that!). They assume that they are the most important and unforgettable persons that ever entered your life, and as a mediator you will never dissuade them of this notion. Again showing my age, think of Ed McMahon, the announcer and armor carrier for Johnny Carson on *The Tonight Show*. Ed would dutifully guffaw at any lame joke or comment uttered by a guest—or even by Johnny—and otherwise subordinate himself to others on the set for the sake of the flow of the show. As a mediator, you will often have to grind your teeth and smile when a lawyer assumes you remember every fact of his last mediation with you from a decade ago, or when he announces that "you're really going to earn your fees today," or when he condescendingly proclaims that "now I'm going to tell you the truth (what was he telling me before this?)." You will all but develop a TMJ disorder in controlling your response when he offers up defenses like "he should have honked before he let my client rear-end him." I have come to refer to this saber-rattling, venting stage of a mediation as The Running of the Bullshit—not in Pamplona, but in a caucus room. And you as the mediator must wear the white clothing and red sash to keep the bull at bay.

Speaking of bull analogies, the middle caucus sessions might require you to transform into a rodeo clown, diverting the bull's attention from others to yourself in a valiant and concerted effort to keep building momentum. Many times you are the messenger to be killed as you are tasked with bringing in a disappointing response to the other room. This requires the skillful ability to "frame" what will doubtlessly be an unwelcome position. More on this important process in chapter 12.

In the later caucuses, the parties have felt they have been heard, and you have inculcated in them the necessary trust in you to allow you to emerge as an agent of reality concerning some obstacles to settlement. Think of yourself as the comedian Paula Poundstone, who, when her mother told her that her own parents taught her to swim by pushing her off a boat, answered, "Mom, maybe they weren't teaching you to swim."

Sometimes I will call on my own experiences as a parable of unrealistic positions. For example, I might talk about my late basset hound Martha, whose every instinct urged her to chase down and pounce upon any duck within view. As she grew accustomed to our daily walks, Martha would be on my leash as we approached a flock of mallards. Those ducks could all but cross her path and peck her on the nose without as much as an acknowledgment from her as she looked straight ahead. Why? Because by then it was more comforting for her dignity to ignore the very existence of the ducks than to humiliate herself yet again by trying in futility to chase them with her short, stubby legs. Parties do the same with disturbing crucial issues.

One mediator well known to me seems to cross the line in his use of analogies for reality checks. He has been said to compare a party's unrealistic demand to "wanting to be in the back seat with the head cheerleader." One can only hope that this mediator's parties abided by the rules of confidentiality. As a father of two daughters and four granddaughters, I don't believe this particular analogy would be either desirable or faithful to my own mediation style. Do not get me wrong. I have been known to be as tacky as anyone. Sometimes I have asked an unrealistic party if she works at Bed, Bath and Beyond—in the "Beyond" department. In the end, however, you can only be yourself and remain faithful to your beliefs in this important role.

In the last caucus stages, as settlement looms as a real possibility, you may wear the hat of an old-time taffy maker, who s-t-r-e-t-c-h-e-s the taffy just far enough, but not too far, lest it break apart. Or you may be the air traffic controller, guiding and timing those crucial last movements to assure an orderly and safe landing. It is at this stage that certain important settlement techniques such as hypothetical "floats," and others to be discussed later, must be deftly applied.

## Ever the Optimist

On repeated occasions, in the middle of a mediation, I have walked into a caucus room to be instantly greeted with, "Uh-oh. You're not smiling." My usual response is *not* "What's there to smile about?" Instead, I will apologize, smile, and explain that I was just lost in my thoughts or concentrating—and that I cannot multi-task. A good and effective mediator remains upbeat and encouraging, exuding enthusiasm and determination that spreads to the participants. Let me share a few of my favorite examples of that innate trait.

After the tragedy that was Hurricane Katrina, I was perusing the New Orleans newspaper and was struck by a caption entitled "76-year-old man survives Katrina alone for 18 days." Below it was a picture of an emaciated man on a rescue gurney, holding a bottle of water as a FEMA team flocked around him. The summary below the picture (we will use a fictitious name) read as follows:

> FEMA workers transport 76-year-old [John Smith], who was found Friday alone in his attic. He says he survived 18 days at his home in New Orleans' 8th Ward with no food, no human contact and only a gallon-and-a-half of water, which ran out Thursday. [Smith] said his family left before the storm, but he stayed to attend church. He later took a nap and says that when he woke up, his house was filling with water. Despite losing a lot of weight, Smith is philosophical. He told rescuers, "So far, so good."

I am an avid reader of history, from which come the following further examples. In 480 BCE, an enormous army of invading Persians was approaching a narrow mountain pass in Greece known as Thermopylae, where a small group of Spartans, led by Dioneces, would make their last stand. A scout dispatched by him returned with the sobering report that "when the Persians shoot forth their arrows, the sun will be darkened by their multitude." Immediately, Dioneces is said to have replied,

> Our friend brings us great tidings! If the Persians darken the sun, we shall have our fight in the shade.

And one more example, featuring the heroic and formidable undertaking that was the Lewis and Clark expedition to find a northwest water passage to the Pacific. After struggling through many months of uncharted and unanticipated weather, terrain, and constant threatening challenges from native American tribes, the group first lay eyes upon the formidable physical and psychological wall that was the Rocky Mountains ahead of them. Merriwether Lewis's first reaction was insightful of his never-say-die mentality so crucial to the mission's ultimate success:

> As I have always held it a crime to anticipate evils, I will believe it to be a good and comfortable road until I am compelled to believe differently.

As a mediator, when handed as you will be a bag of lemons, you must find the nearest glass pitcher and some ice cubes and transform it into a refreshing and thirst-quenching lemonade. And when half of it has been consumed, you must praise the fact that the pitcher remains not half empty, but half full.

## An Unfailing Sense of Humor

This quality is so immensely important to a mediator that it merits its own chapter.

Chapter 3

# Weapons of Mass Distraction

---

Take my stress. Please. Repeatedly, studies and surveys of the prime quality reported by clients that elevated a good mediator into an outstanding one was a timely sense of humor—with the emphasis on timing. The immortal Groucho Marx recognized the therapeutic effect of his profession almost 100 years ago:

> A clown is like an aspirin—only he works twice as fast.

Scientific studies have repeatedly verified this phenomenon. Dr. Michael Miller and associates at the University of Maryland School of Medicine studied the process of vasodilation, the ability of your blood vessels to expand. The wider the vessel, the greater the blood flow to the brain. The greater the blood flow, the more positive and constructive the subject's outlook. They chose a control group of some 40 college students, separating them into screening rooms of 20 apiece. One room was shown the opening sequence of the movie *Saving Private Ryan*, the D-Day beach landing with all its gore and chaos. The other room was shown an identically long segment from *Kingpin*, a Bill Murray film chock full of one-liners, pratfalls, and silliness. Each group's blood vessels were then measured. Of the 20 in the *Private Ryan* room, 14 displayed constriction of their vessels, with an average of 35 percent less blood flow to the brain. In contrast, fully 19 of 20 *Kingpin* watchers exhibited dilated vessels, an average 22 percent increase in blood flow.

Anecdotally, Norman Cousins, longtime beloved editor of *Saturday Review*, wrote about being diagnosed with a debilitating, crippling case of arthritis in the 1960s. He tried all that medical science had to offer with little or no relief. In desperation, he went home and fed himself a steady diet of Marx Brothers movies, and soon his recovery was palpable. His detailed account, *Anatomy of an Illness*, became a bestseller in 1979.

More and more medical institutions are making this important connection. A children's hospital in Chicago for a decade staffed a "humor cart" laden with gag toys and jokey doodads, with a trained attendant who made rounds with a single goal—to elicit a small giggle from an infirm child. The indirect goal was to decrease the child's anxiety, making his body less likely to resist treatment. One insightful attendant described it as "the element of forgetting where we are."

So how do all of these comedic building blocks apply to a structured, concentrated negotiation such as your typical mediation? You begin with the premise that many participants in this exercise (especially plaintiffs in personal injury cases, many of whom are new to the process) are either very angry and/or fearful as they enter a negotiation. For them, it is anything but "another day at the office." Any mediator worth her salt knows that unless you can peel away the armor of resentment and fear in your participants, you are doomed to failure. In essence, humor helps to cut through the emotional roadblocks, which are kryptonite to the rational and productive collaboration so essential to reaching a consensus.

As a mediator, I frequently resorted to what I call S&M tactics. No, my techniques rarely involved whips, chains, or handcuffs, though the occasional medieval weapon might have been in order. My S&M stood for Sarcasm and Mockery, and it took many forms, depending on a myriad of personalities and circumstances. I have used props such as a Magic 8-Ball that when shaken would divine varying fortunes, and fortune cookies that led to absurd conclusions and comic relief. I gained a reputation for using classic recycled cartoons with my own self-styled captions that assisted me in reality checks, as well as not-so-subtle anecdotes that used gallows humor to convey the message that at the end, we are all in this lifeboat together rocked by a vast and unpredictable ocean. I could quote the headstone of W.C. Fields ("On the whole, I'd rather be in Philadelphia") or of a detested British serial killer on his way to the gallows ("Are you sure this thing is safe?"). Or during a downtime, I could cite a comedian's line about his grandfather's death ("When I die, I want to go peacefully in my sleep, like my grandfather—not screaming like the passengers in his car.")

Early in my career I recognized the value of dark humor, as described by the great Mel Brooks ("Tragedy is when I cut off my finger. Comedy is when you fall in a manhole and die."). Sarcasm to a receptive subject can work wonders ("The clueless store called. They're outta you."), and self-effacement was always a favorite, inspired by the master, Rodney Dangerfield ("My wife loves to talk to me during sex. Just yesterday, she called me from a Motel 6."). At times, I might have noted in passing that I had to play the village idiot in the other room, "which comes quite naturally to me." All of these techniques helped build camaraderie and rapport if used appropriately.

On some occasions, the participants themselves either intentionally or accidentally would add to the comedy, as when one plaintiff, obviously impressed by my incredible knowledge and wisdom, declared that I was "a real suppository of information."

But alas, timing is everything, and ill-timed humor in a mediation can set off a conflagration that is virtually inextinguishable. The effective mediator is, in essence, as much of a mood scientist—indeed, a mood *changer*—as your standard issue stand-up comedian in a dark smoke-filled cabaret. Both of our professions rely heavily on improvisation, and face the unsettling consequences of audience rejection. And at the end of the day, we both work exceedingly hard to sow the seeds of a therapeutic snicker, and pray the hecklers stay away.

While on the subject of comedians, I was privileged in my practice to conduct scores of mediations involving an insurance claims man who moonlighted as a Cajun comedian. This was an occupation he did not like to divulge in our mediations, though his friendly and affable mediation style made him a natural in both fields. His secret was safe with me, until one day providence prevailed. Late in a mediation, I presented the insurance company's possible final offer to the plaintiff's attorney (whose surname coincidentally could well have originated "down on the bayou"). Laughing sarcastically, he uttered the rhetorical question, "Who is this guy—some sort of comedian?" I couldn't resist with an honest answer, combined with an off-the-cuff promise that if he came down just a little on his demand, I could get the adjuster a little higher—and have him perform his favorite Cajun joke as lagniappe. The adjuster was far from amused when I meekly announced my unauthorized entreaty, but was charmed just enough to "humor me." The case settled, and he entered the plaintiff's room and dutifully gave a masterful rendition of an Alphonse and Clotilde joke, much to the delight of all present. As everyone was leaving, however, he took me aside and politely requested that I never again give away his valuable inventory. In all our future mediations, I respected his wishes and resorted to other cheap tricks in my arsenal to help settle his cases.

Chapter 4

# Prepping the Roux

---

Your job as a mediator starts long before you arrive at the situs of the mediation. On receipt of an inquiry or assignment, I typically would send a letter or email to all counsel confirming the date, time, and place of the mediation and thanking them for choosing me. I would then disclose any known potential personal or professional conflict either with any party or with counsel that could possibly create an appearance of impropriety in my acting as a neutral in the case (see further discussion on this issue in chapter 9). I would inform them that I would assume that no conflict existed, or that if any existed, it was waived by all parties unless I received a written objection within a week of my transmission. My missive would also confirm the allocation of mediation fees among the parties. I also included language requesting that counsel make their best effort to have all decision makers present or at least available remotely for the mediation. My next request would be that all parties supplement prior discovery and/or update any significant medical or economic issue enough in advance of the mediation as to be susceptible to review and consideration by decision makers. I then would request that if the parties deemed it appropriate, confidential position papers be submitted to me at least 48 hours prior to the mediation, noting that the papers need only include basic facts of the case and any information or documents that each felt would be useful to me in helping them resolve the case. Lastly, I reminded counsel that I was reserving my entire day for this mediation (unless a half-day mediation was set), and implored them that if for any reason the mediation would not proceed as scheduled, I be notified of this as soon as they knew. This submission was important for several reasons.

As to the allocation of mediation fees, experience taught me that the last thing a mediator wants is to be held in suspension on payment with lawyers appearing at mediation and declaring that the allocation would be decided at the end of the day. You do not want parties failing to reach a mediated settlement to then vent their frustration on how the mediator should be paid. Many mediation services prepare a mediation contract containing the fee basis and allocation that is circulated for execution by all parties at the opening joint session. More on this topic will be discussed in the next chapter.

Attendance and participation of decision makers at mediation is important on several fronts. The attendance by a personal injury plaintiff is usually, but not always, a given. There are exceptions. I recall one matter several years ago when I was informed by plaintiff's counsel in confidence beforehand that his client could not participate "live" in the mediation because he had recently been imprisoned. We informed the defendants that although plaintiff was "out of pocket," he would be calling in to listen to the opening session and would be available to speak to me and his counsel as the day went on. No, I did not say he was "detained," but after some minor protesting by defense counsel, the matter went off without a hitch and the case settled. In another case, the plaintiff's counsel warned me that his client, suffering from agoraphobia, emotionally was unable to sit in a room with several people. Yes, the subsequent reality check discussion with his counsel of how his client would manage to sit in a courtroom for several days in front of 12 strangers was low-hanging fruit for any mediator. Nevertheless, with this confidential information in hand, we allowed his counsel to declare that plaintiff was not feeling well, but was available in an adjoining room for brief private audiences. The matter proceeded to settlement.

Additionally, as a mediator you want to do your best to assure that even non-party influencers are present or at least participate in the mediation. The last thing you need, as happened to me, is to have an absent non-lawyer boyfriend veto a prospective settlement at the end of the day because he had seen a much higher recovery recently for a similar injury on *The People's Court*. Even if unpleasant, surly, or unreasonable, you want these persons invested in the mediation, listening to both the good and bad points of the case before they help advise their significant other.

In the defense room, the main issue is that of bureaucratic unavailability. Many insurers are regionalizing to offices far from a mediation site. It is a fact of modern insurance life that many claims adjusters have hundreds of files, making it more difficult to personally attend every mediation. If you are apprised of this impossibility, my advice is to persuade the defense to send someone—a human being, and hopefully not a professional actor—to the mediation to avoid the appearance that the parties are not on a level playing field, with plaintiff taking the time to be there but defendants leaving an empty chair. I would further strongly advise the defense to arrange for a decision maker to participate at least remotely in the opening session (and hope he or she is not playing solitaire at the same time). The committed availability of "The Wizard of Oz" behind the curtain is a crucial perception in a mediation. As bad as "good cop, bad cop" tactics may be, they are far preferable to "good cop, uninterested cop." Lastly, provisions should be made for availability of corporate decision makers who may be in a different time zone. Eastern time is enough of a challenge for those in Central or Pacific time zone mediations. London time is anathema.

The exceptional circumstances of social distancing required by the COVID-19 pandemic have deeply affected the ability to have face-to-face mediations. As an alternative, many parties have resorted to online substitutes in an effort to salvage mediation dates and settle cases. While I acknowledge this necessity on a Plan B basis, my concern is that these methods will become more and more acceptable and institutionalized. I strongly believe that such distant negotiations lose much in translating emotions and feelings that are best digested and dealt with in a "live" venue. Continuing the analogy of a mediator to a stand-up comedian, the latter's worst nightmare is to have his audience sitting too far away. No connection is possible. So it is also with a mediator.

Lien holder resolution or participation also is important. Among these, your biggest challenge is usually the workers' compensation benefits intervenor. In a humor piece written many years ago, I referred to their counsel as the "pariahs of litigation." Much like the nerdy pledges directed to the back room in *National Lampoon's Animal House*, they are traditionally relegated to the slum districts of mediation venues, be they dark hallways, coat closets, supply rooms, or judges' kitchens. Their tale of woe is that ironically their clients are the first to pay and the last to recover. Outraged demands by plaintiff lawyers that an intervenor not only waive his lien but also throw in "new money" to the settlement pot are looked upon by the intervenor's counsel with incredulous disdain. But be mindful that under laws of certain states, intervenors get the last laugh, because it is next to impossible to settle a case without their approval, and those settlements are entitled to the dreaded "dollar for dollar" credit on any future benefits due. Thankfully, at the end of the day the parties may have a crumb thrown their way by intervenor's counsel, a reduction in the lien by more than the contingency attorney's fees percentage in exchange for a full and final release of future workers' compensation liability. But an unwritten rule of workers' compensation intervenors is that only their lawyers may participate in a mediation, and that all efforts to reach their own "Wizard of Oz," or ultimate authority, are futile.

Concerning the request for position papers, you will find many times that present-day insurers refuse to pay their lawyers for this endeavor, in which case you will not receive one from their counsel. When you do receive them, you will often find that they arrive at closing time the day before the mediation or even on the morning of the proceeding. More on this in chapter 10. For now, the short message is to cowboy (or cowgirl) up and read and digest them. And while I'm venting about these submissions, the following collection of items submitted to me is proof positive that some lawyers may not be paying close attention to what they submit. Consider:

- Plaintiff's wife is also making her own claim for loss of *contortion*.
- Plaintiff claims he cannot maintain an erection because of pain in his low back ... He should think *long and hard* before asserting this (if he could do that, we wouldn't be discussing this ...).
- Our economist fixed the total income loss to the end of our client's *wormlife* expectancy.
- When *martial* relations are engaged in by plaintiff and his wife ...

- Claimant asserts low back and right-sided *legal* pain ...
- She has difficulty doing typical household tasks such as vacuuming, sweeping, and *moping*.
- An MRI of his back confirmed an indented *fecal* sac ...

The request for updating discovery responses or any significant medical or economic issue is an effort to avoid last-minute mediation surprises that make it next to impossible to resolve a case. One glaring example early in my career involved a plaintiff who had sustained a comminuted leg fracture that had required several surgeries. That we could all prepare for. But imagine the looks in the eyes of the defendants when plaintiff arrived at the mediation fresh off an undisclosed thigh-level amputation. We all left very early that day.

Pre-mediation preparation and confidential discussions can even prove to be potential life savers. In one matter that was scheduled for mediation in central Louisiana, the defense lawyer informed me that a review of plaintiff's medical records had revealed an evaluation by a treating psychologist that his patient was known to carry weapons and was capable of using them "in times of stress." This caused us to be proactive in advance of the mediation, with defense lawyer retaining a trusted (and armed) retired local police officer to sit in on the mediation. He was never introduced to the plaintiff, but appeared in a coat and tie and blended in with the defense group without saying a word. His orders were to shoot first and ask questions later if plaintiff as much as made a hasty move for anything hidden. Fast-forward to the near conclusion of the mediation, when Monopoly money numbers were all used up and The Dance was proceeding to Spotlight Time. Oftentimes this stage of a mediation has been known to be somewhat stressful, with a dash of fatigue thrown in. For some reason long forgotten, I had gathered the entire group back together and suddenly, with nary a word said, the plaintiff arose mysteriously and methodically exited the conference room and walked to the parking lot, where from the cab of his pickup truck he retrieved an ominous-looking bag. He then re-entered our meeting and placed the bag on his lap. As most of us stared expectantly at the well-dressed ex-cop, plaintiff slooooowly (probably saving untold carnage) pulled out a weathered King James edition bible, where he had kept, for sacred safekeeping, his treasured picture of the Harley he intended to buy with his take-home from the settlement proceeds. Crisis averted.

By all means, read all that is submitted to you, and make a pre-mediation outline that can be used in validating the parties' positions and in displaying your preparation and understanding of the basic issues in the case. This simple act will help confirm the fact that you arrived at the mediation committed to the process.

Lastly, if the mediation involves counsel or parties who know you well, you might briefly contact them beforehand to request that they limit affable contact with you during the mediation, or risk damaging your role as a neutral to others participating who have never met you before that day.

## Chapter 5

# We Are All Gathered Here Today ...

---

All of us know that the typical mediation is composed of an opening, or "joint," session attended by all participants, followed by as many private caucuses as may be required. At times, thinking outside the lines, you may need to have another joint session on a particular issue that may have come up, or a session involving only the attorneys, but always with consent of the parties.

Before delving into the dynamics of the joint session, let us identify at least five types of negotiating styles exhibited by lawyers or their clients:

1. *The Fighter*—Rambo personified. Win at all costs. Withhold information, stretch the facts, and take no prisoners.
2. *The Appeaser*—Think President Jimmy Carter in the 1970s. Kindly, cooperative, realistic, accepts his weak points and listens well.
3. *The Distractor*—This is the Houdini of negotiators. Now you see an argument, now you don't. Tries to change horses at mid-stream. Frustratingly non-committal.

4. *The Analyst*—Extremely left-brained. He dissects everything. Makes huge issues about minute discrepancies. Prepare for a long mediation.
5. *The Idealist*—This is the crusader for Truth and Justice. Vendettas prevail. Everything is a matter of principle.

One central purpose of the joint session is to give you as mediator the first chance to discern what types of negotiators you will be dealing with that day. It enables you to tactfully begin defusing damaging styles with your own well-chosen opening remarks in the joint session.

At times, lawyers will approach you requesting that the joint session be waived. They may say that the parties are too emotional or that it just wastes time, since everyone knows the issues. I resist this move for several important reasons. If the lawyers persist, I usually am successful in at least convincing them to let us conduct a brief session where only I will be required to speak. At its core, the joint session, with everyone gathered together, is a great opportunity for me as mediator to set the tone for the day as one of cooperation and communal spirit in working together to resolve this dispute. Without engaging in sacrilege, envision The Last Supper (hopefully *sans* Judas). It further allows me to sell myself as a mediator to those who have never worked with me and sell the process to those who question its benefits.

As stated before, every mediator has to be herself, and your presentation in a joint session may differ widely from mine. Although you will find yourself varying these comments depending on your audience or the facts of the case, my general opening comments begin with a request that everyone around the table execute a mediation contract that includes the pre-mediation agreement on fee allocation as well as confidentiality language. A practical effect of this document is its future use during the day as a cheat sheet for me as to the names of all parties participating. This is particularly useful in multi-party cases. Incidentally, I will ask that parties both print and sign their names. At times I explain this by remarking that we need this because lawyers all took a class in law school to make their signatures illegible. If someone has a problem with the fee allocation or wishes to postpone that decision, I will announce that after the joint session is complete I will step outside for five minutes and allow them to finalize this issue among themselves, because we have far more important matters to spend our time on today.

As this document is circulating for signatures, I will ask that all participants around the table introduce themselves, if need be. I will introduce myself last, and often begin my drive to help forge a cooperative spirit by highlighting matters that all parties agree upon. For example, in a death case, where emotions are rightfully raw and on the surface, I might tell everyone that we may disagree on many things that day, but that I am certain we all agree on at least two fundamental facts—that what happened on the day of the accident was a tragedy, and that no one wishes to be here as a result of that tragedy. I will then typically begin with self-effacing comments such as the fact that in my career I tried cases in some 27 courts and left disappointed in 26 of them, except for the courthouse in little Leesville, Louisiana, where I was unbeaten—because I tried only one case there and refused thereafter ever to return so as to keep my perfect record intact somewhere. I am not shy about stealing others' material, and might proceed with a cohort's analogy of courtrooms not being cathedrals where justice is done, but rather casinos where dice get rolled. Continuing the reality check theme, I may mention that in a jury trial your fate will be decided by 12 strangers, 11 of whom are already aggravated because they did not know anyone who could get them out of jury duty, and a twelfth one, who had a secret agenda that could do grievous harm to any of the parties around the room. I might even quote the famous line by Mike Tyson in responding to a forthcoming boxing opponent's plan to beat him:

> Everybody's got a plan—'til they get punched in the face.

I then will stress that today is a day of sharing information and of the singular opportunity to resolve this matter while the parties can still control their own fate.

Next, I will state one or two ground rules for my mediation. One is that I am free to share any information given to me in a caucus unless I am told to keep it private, and if so, any secret is safe with me. If I am feeling feisty, or am with familiar litigants, I might add that the main rule is to laugh uproariously at my jokes, or it will cost them dearly. Or I might tell them to pace themselves, because no one is allowed to settle before they are served lunch—or even better, post-lunch snacks. All of this is designed to help clear the air of counterproductive tension and set the tone for the parties' presentation.

Usually the lawyers do all the talking on behalf of the parties, and most do a good job, again depending on their negotiating style. No one on my watch ever uttered the words "moron," or "weasel," or "scoundrel," or "ho." There was, however, one occasion in a matter involving major credibility issues where the defense lawyer arose after the plaintiff's presentation, looked disdainfully at him, and said, "You, sir, are a damned liar." Matters got out of hand soon thereafter, causing me to have to physically restrain the plaintiff before I ushered defense counsel out of the room. When I asked him sardonically if that tactic ever worked for him in any past mediation, he matter-of-factly responded that he felt the plaintiff needed "some shock and awe." After a long day, the matter settled, but no one shook hands.

Other defense lawyers have good intentions with damaging results, such as one who addressed the plaintiff with the assurance that this matter had been carefully "round tabled" by his insurance client's committee at their home office, and that "at the end of the day, we will be making you a very reasonable offer." Of course, the problem with these well-intended reassurances was in giving the perception that the defense position was set in stone long before the mediation, making negotiation that day seem like a one-way street. Not surprisingly, the plaintiff in the very first caucus told me, "If they're waiting all day to make me a reasonable offer, just make it now and let's decide if it's worth staying."

The most effective lawyer presentations are those that make their position in unemotional fashion, and say something to the effect that they do not expect that day to convince the opposing parties, but are confident that they can convince a jury. They follow that by sending the message that their client is nevertheless there to listen to all sides, as long as opposing parties are as well.

As a bilingual mediator, I have often been selected to preside in cases where a party (usually an injured plaintiff) does not have grasp of the English language. In one notable case, the injured lady brought along her son to help her translate and explain the proceedings. After my opening remarks and those of her lawyer, the defense lawyer spoke in English about some of the liability issues in the case as the woman looked at her son for a translation. He turned to her and I overheard him whisper to her in Spanish, "The lawyer says they're not going to offer you any money." This was in fact a gigantic mischaracterization of what the lawyer had said, and I was forced smilingly to spring to action with a more accurate translation.

Although lawyers typically discourage their clients from speaking in a joint session, I will usually encourage their participation, as long as civility prevails. Indeed, a client's face-to-face telling of their story to the opposition can help relieve them of their emotional need to retell their story in the courtroom. One particular occasion bears retelling. The plaintiff's attorney had contacted my office on mediation day to advise that the scheduled start of the mediation would be slightly delayed that morning. He added that he would explain the reason when he arrived with his client. A few minutes later, in they walked. The client was a charming and spirited elderly lady, retired after decades of dedicated service as a school teacher. She seemed a bit stressed. We made her comfortable in her private caucus room before inviting her lawyer to my office to get "the rest of the story." Apparently, the client, who was asserting that the accident being mediated had caused a severe cervical injury with related numbness down her left arm, had been rear-ended earlier that very morning on the way to meet her lawyer to prepare for the mediation. To his credit, he disclosed to me that he had had a frank discussion with his client and that while they certainly would not lie, they also would not voluntarily disclose to the opposition that day what had happened barely an hour ago. He also mentioned that his client had had another vehicular accident after the accident sued upon, and that since defendants were already aware of that one, he would cover it in the opening session of the mediation.

We proceeded to the opening session. The plaintiff's counsel was impeccable and eloquent in advocating his client's case. Then he did something that most of his cohorts would hesitate doing. Concluding his opening remarks by mentioning the previously disclosed subsequent accident, he smiled at defense lawyer and at his adjuster and declared, "Now, we know and acknowledge that you have an issue with another accident my client was involved in. We are not here to play hide-the-ball with that. Mrs. Jones, why don't you tell these folks in your own words about that accident?" She innocently looked back at him and before you could say "strike three," the kindly lady said, "Oh, you mean the one today? He hit me really hard!" With a nervous grin, her able lawyer shifted seamlessly into major Damage Control Mode as defense counsel and adjuster all but needed bibs to stem their anticipatory drooling. A few hours later, the parties settled their case for a surprisingly tidy sum, and I was convinced the adjuster had rewarded Mrs. Jones's disarming honesty and spunk.

In summary, do not overlook the importance of the joint session as an important vehicle in setting the proper stage for more substantive discussions in the caucus process.

## Chapter 6

# The Early Caucuses: "I *Think* I Can ..."

---

After the joint session, I usually call for a five-minute break to allow bathroom trips and, most importantly, let the parties privately discuss what went on in the session and get their bearings before I commence to meet confidentially with them. Typically, I will meet in the plaintiff's room first—but there are exceptions.

Periodically, in cases that involve multiple defendants, I will perceive from the position papers or from the joint session that the defendants are about to get off to a threatening start by playing the "who flinches first" game among themselves, resulting in a combined opening defense offer that portends a lack of respect for the process. I have been known on those occasions to seize credibility in my return visit to the plaintiff room by remarking offhandedly that the defendants "are pissing on your shoes and calling it a rain shower." If I can see this bad start coming, then at the conclusion of the joint session I will try to head it off by requesting permission from plaintiff and her counsel to meet very briefly first with the defense group. Normally they will not object to this. When I enter the defense room (each of whose representatives has a death grip on his wallet), I will often quote Ben Franklin's advice to the colonies:

We must all hang together, or assuredly we shall all hang separately.

I then suggest to them that no opening offer ever settles a case, and that the worst thing they can do is hold the plaintiff hostage or get off to a horrible start by combining meager numbers that produce an offensive opening offer. Instead, I leave them with a homework assignment while I try to get into the plaintiff's room as quickly as possible. Their charge is to jointly determine what a reasonable opening offer would be, and not to waste valuable time in determining which defendant would fund what percentage, since the opening number will certainly not settle the case. Indeed, half seriously I guarantee them that if the opening offer does settle the matter, I will volunteer to arbitrate funding percentages among the defendants—for free.

The majority of the time, my first caucus visit is in the plaintiff's room. Many times, the plaintiff has never before been in this position and looks askance at me and at the process. This is where I try to produce an atmosphere of this room as a sanctuary: one of safety, proactive listening, and rapport. The last thing a mediator wants to do in an opening caucus is to argue with a plaintiff and put her on the defense. Empathy and compassion are keys. The primary focus is to allow venting, and to ask questions that show you are interested in understanding her position. Sometimes at the conclusion of an opening caucus I might tell the plaintiff that today is about three plans:

Plan A: To settle this case if we can.

Plan B: To settle this case if we can.

Plan C: If settlement options are disappointing, at least exchange as much information throughout the day to allow an intelligent decision.

At times, a plaintiff's opening caucus results in an opening demand that is unrealistic at best. The worst are those that "move the goalposts" from pre-mediation discussions without prior notice to the defendants. This tactic gravely threatens an early conclusion to your mediation. On one occasion, with a straight face, I asked plaintiff's lawyer to help me how to go into the defense room and justify that a case he represented last week to be worth $250,000 was now worth double that amount. Ever so condescendingly, he tutored me on the process: "Tell them that was a settlement demand. This is a mediation demand." I did not argue at this point, but left him with an early but tactful reality check cartoon. One of my favorites is a *Far Side* cartoon depicting a nerdy youngster trying to coax a turtle to leap through a flaming hoop ("Through the hoop, Ernie, through the hoop!"), or I might flash a smile and quote another Yogi-ism ("It's getting late early.").

So other than wearing sufficient armor to gird one's loins, what does one do in presenting such an opening plaintiff demand in the defense room? As with unrealistic opening defense positions, I certainly do not endorse or justify this rubbish. After listening to defense's venting, I try to persuade the defendant to stay the course, and not to succumb to a tempting responsive number that says, "You've just shown me the sun, so I'll show you the moon." I may discuss the real phenomenon that whoever first seizes credibility usually ends with the better deal in a negotiation—and I suggest that defendant make the same opening offer he would make even if plaintiff had made a more reasonable opening demand. The goal is to send the plaintiff the message of where defense will not go by way of subsequent offers made in the caucus process, based upon the exchange of sufficient information to allow a rational evaluation in both rooms of the parties' positions.

If defense resists making a realistic opening offer, I do my best to convince them that I will bring that number to the plaintiff's room—but that two numbers from now I really will need the defense to be at a significantly higher number (and I then name the number), or risk threatening my own credibility in the plaintiff's room and hence the entire mediation. I then follow this up in the plaintiff's room by preaching to her that if she makes a realistic response to an admittedly disappointing defense number, I am confident it will be appreciated and rewarded very soon in the defense room.

Often a defendant will factor in questionable liability or comparative fault issues to drastically reduce an opening offer that would not even cover plaintiff's expenses. One way to frame such a disappointing number in the plaintiff's room is to focus on the number being offered, arguing that if defense has evaluated damages at a sufficiently high range, it matters not at the end of the day if a reduction percentage on that gross number is applied. The net return could well be either the same or so close as to be irrelevant. The slice-of-pie analogy is frequently helpful. If the pie is bigger than expected, who cares if a small slice is removed to save face?

At times, a defendant will want to use "smoking guns" too early in the process, when emotions in the plaintiff's room are still raw. These may take the form of filmed activity checks or undisclosed prior or subsequent accidents or even criminal convictions. My usual advice is to save these bullets for much later in the process, when both parties have made progress and the prospect of a settlement looms on the horizon.

Your goal as a mediator in early caucuses is to at least allow the ship to leave the dock and enter blue waters on the way to its port, wherever that may be.

One of my favorite episodes of the old *Seinfeld* comedy series was when the character Kramer is burned by a cup of latte and retains counsel to sue the manufacturer. As he and his counsel are driving to an initial settlement meeting at the defendant's corporate office, Kramer's lawyer warns him to keep his mouth shut and let him do the talking. As they enter the office, the defense representative, after a few pleasantries, mentions that her client discussed the possibility of showing its good will by offering Kramer free lifetime latte and ... before she finishes her sentence, Kramer jumps up and yells, "I'll take it!" His lawyer is crushed. The point of repeating this hilarious scene is that there exists such an animal as "The Winner's Curse." In effect, a deal done too quickly, and without sufficient negotiation, gives the parties the feeling that perhaps substantial concessions were left on the negotiation table. Better to let the numbers simmer.

As we advance into late early, or early middle, caucuses, your job as a mediator is to continue engendering faith in your commitment and expertise, while keeping the process fun. At times, before I leave a caucus room I may ask the parties there to each independently write on a folded piece of paper what they believe the other side's next offer might be, with the closest winning my next cartoon. I tell them we don't play "The Price Is Right" rules, and the closest wins, even if it's above the actual number. My goal then is to surprise them with (in the plaintiff's room) a higher number than the room anticipated, or (in the defense room) a larger reduction. I may call on this dividend of confidence in me later in the mediation when I might ask one room or the other to respond with a lower (or higher) number than they were comfortable with. I have been known at that point to declare in jest, "I am a trained professional—do not try this at home."

This mid caucus process continues with the intent of "funneling," where the issues continue to narrow to one or two central areas that now become manageable. And all along the way, I continue trying to make the process as fun and enjoyable as possible with tactful but effective reality checks. One favorite is to announce to the parties in the room that you will hold up for them for 30 seconds a sheet of paper containing a single sentence that has a certain number of Fs. They are to secretly and independently count the Fs and then independently announce the number in the room. The sentence can be something like:

> Two of the most powerful and effective of all human fears are fear of failure and the fear of success.

I have yet to encounter a room where in that short time span, all participants (or even most) have arrived at the correct answer: 11 Fs. This leads naturally to a discussion of how human beings, even intelligent ones, will have vastly varying perceptions, and that it just might be that 12 of them on a jury will decide their fate.

I might also summon another *Far Side* cartoon, depicting a western fort under siege by native Americans, who obviously are winning the battle against the fort's defenders. One of them has removed a note from an arrow sticking in the back of his dying cohort, and mockingly declares, "Ha! The idiots spelled 'surrender' with only one 'r'!"

Another favorite is a *New Yorker* courtroom cartoon depicting a dog as the litigating party facing a jury of 12 cats ("What kind of jury will YOU get?").

A healthy smattering of fun but pointed reality checks is a useful tool during this exercise in tactfully helping parties come to their senses.

Often in these middle caucuses, when multiple defendants are involved, if you are getting disappointing joint movement and suspect one or two of them are to blame, you might separate them into their own rooms. This helps to avert the "herd" mentality, a process where all defendants cheer themselves into defiant positions. When separated, you might plant the seed of doubt with some of the most recalcitrant parties that there is a real possibility that unilateral settlements might be made by some of the more motivated defendants that just might leave them as The Last of the Mohicans in a hostile courtroom.

Sometimes mid-caucus impasses can be caused by the lawyers rather than their clients. If you find yourself being bombarded with beverages each time I enter your caucus room, it's because I am hoping that sooner rather than later your bladder will cause you to leave the room. When this happens, I may "accidentally" accost you in a hallway and talk to you like the classic Dutch uncle.

On other occasions, a lawyer's own need for venting of his position might be inhibiting progress that should have materialized by the middle caucuses. Here is an example that I encountered years ago. This plaintiff's lawyer was renowned for his quick temper sprinkled with large doses of arrogance. That day his co-counsel was his current wife. The defense lawyer was experienced and even-tempered, accompanied by his client rep, a nice enough man with a good sense of humor. The case involved an industrial accident where the defendant's scaffold plank had fallen from above, striking the plaintiff, who thankfully was wearing a hard hat. Damages claimed included issues with his cervical spine as well as some rather fuzzy traumatic brain injury issues. After several hours of caucuses, I entered his room with yet another "baby step" defense offer and framed it the best I could. He turned to his co-counsel spouse, instructing her to follow him, and ordered me to come along as well. When we reached the parking lot, he reached his luxury van and warned me to stand aside. He then systematically unloaded a seriously heavy-looking scaffold plank from the rear of his vehicle along with a yellow hard hat. He then told me to put on the hat. There was no mediator language that suitably replaced my reflexive response of, "Not in *this* lifetime, my friend." Acting quite pleased with himself that he had predicted my hesitancy, he then unloaded an empty cardboard storage box and placed it on the pavement. As his wife did her best Vanna White imitation, he balanced the plank on the pavement, then allowed it to tip over and crash into the box, causing it to crater. He then summarily announced to me that I had five minutes to convince the defense group to witness his demonstration, or else he, his wife, and their client were leaving and would proceed to smite them in court. I hurried to the defense room, ignoring expected arguments of the probable courtroom inadmissibility of such a pedestrian test. Luckily, I had worked many times before with this defense counsel, who had learned, right or wrong, to trust me. I asked him and his client to simply follow me to the parking lot and to courteously allow the lawyer to put on his show, but not to say a word. I told them I was confident that their quiet participation in this exercise would soon help me to help them get the case resolved. They did, and soon thereafter serious movement commenced. The matter settled after a few follow-up phone calls the next day.

To summarize, by the end of the middle caucuses, the momentum and optimism in a mediation should be palpable. Like the pilot at 30,000 feet, you should be able to announce to all passengers that we have reached our cruising altitude and that they are free to walk around the cabin.

## Chapter 7

# Late Caucuses: "I *Know* I Can ..."

Hours after the joint session and many private caucuses later, the parties often will vent in frustration that the proverbial well is dry to any further concessions. Oftentimes, by then, the grayish outline of Bali Hai, the land of settlement, beckons alluringly on the horizon. How to get there? You rely on the several past hours in which you painstakingly built a strong foundation. Think of the title of the once popular book by the immortal football coach Vince Lombardi, and *Run to Daylight.* Summon all of the creative, intellectual, optimistic, and competitive instincts within you and "get 'er done."

There are countless closing techniques that you might call on in getting to the promised land. You might well fashion your own. The following is a smattering of some methods that, depending on the circumstances, have helped me along the way.

By now, you know that the effective and timely use of cartoons was part of my "shtick." Never were they more useful than in the tail end of a mediation, when the parties' growing fatigue and frustration is extinguished by a quick dose of humor. In the plaintiff's room, I might summon a favorite *Far Side* cartoon depicting a prehistoric man with "the first kite," a large stone attached to a string. In the defense room, I may resort to the insightful "Peanuts" dialogue between Linus and Lucy:

> Linus: If I stand here long enough, do you think someone will come along and give me a bicycle?
>
> Lucy: I doubt it.
>
> Linus: That's too bad. I like to get things for free.

In my career I collected hundreds of cartoons that proved useful at the right time in a particular mediation. In fact, I would half-jokingly admonish a regular client that if she ever got a repeat cartoon from me, she was probably using me too much.

I often would resort to momentum-inducing analogies to send the message that we were too close to give up now. I might urge that we had already gotten past the twenty-fifth mile in a marathon and had but a few hundred yards to go; or that Neil Diamond was singing "Sweet Caroline" and they were turning the house lights off. In the plaintiff's room, I might focus on the infinitesimally small difference that remained, and wondered whether he would bet that difference on a Las Vegas roulette table and risk losing everything gained that day.

On other occasions, you might call upon your own true combat stories from the courtroom to bring home the fact that strange and tragic results can happen. One of mine was a case involving a kindly little old lady who, during a busy Christmas shopping season in a mall, slipped and fell on something spilled on the floor, resulting in her permanent paralysis. After turning down a seven-figure offer just before trial commenced, she encountered a jury that found her to be solely at fault for her accident, completely dismissing her claim.

If I genuinely felt this way, late in the day I might turn to a mentally exhausted and disappointed plaintiff and tell her that whether we settle or not (and certainly we should), I had appreciated her hard work and felt privileged to have worked with her. This was often met with reciprocal appreciation and a refueling of efforts to conclude a settlement. On one memorable occasion, the plaintiff looked at me and declared in his own poetic way, "You, sir, are an oasis in a sea of bullshit." To this day, I do not quite comprehend the geography of this analogy, but will humbly accept it as an attempted heartfelt compliment.

A technique I have used toward the end of a day involving multiple defendants is one taught to me that involves the use of a calculator. You explain to the defendants that to maintain the confidentiality of their absolutely final respective contributions toward a "pool," you will input a fictitious amount into the calculator. Each defendant then will individually input his or her contribution. The fictitious initial number averts the possibility that any one defendant will know the others' input amount. I then subtract my fictitious number from the joint inputs, and we have a pool of working capital to use in the plaintiff's room.

There are methods that I have used to indirectly obtain an insight as to a party's settlement goal or even his possible bottom line. Incidentally, I will never solicit a party's settlement number until there is absolutely no other option. In my opinion, to do so severely restricts my style and duties as a neutral. One method is to share with one room my "feel" that ultimately the other room might get to a certain number. Note that this is not a breach of confidentiality, since it is only an intelligent projection. I then listen to and observe intently the room's reaction to my projection, both verbally and in their body language.

Another offshoot of this method, or even a follow-up to my projected number, is to inquire of the party what *she* thinks the other room came with. More often than not, this response strongly tracks what her own settlement position might be, or else arguably she would not still be in the mediation.

Yet another method of indirect settlement number divination is the use of a "bracket" procedure. To the uninformed, this is a method whereby one room declares that if the other room will offer a certain proposed number, they will counter with another stated number. Typically these numbers represent an attempt to accelerate the pace of negotiation to a midpoint number. I have often preached to parties that the problem with presenting a bracket to the other room in this way is the all-too-real phenomenon of "reactive devaluation." This means that a party generally will respond negatively to any proposal made by the other room. What I encourage parties to do is, rather than announcing the proposed bracket as their own proposal, to allow me to go to the other room and suggest that *I* as a mediator may be able to convince the parties in the other room to jump-start the process with a "leap of faith" number—but that reading between the lines, it will probably require this room to reward that promising number with its own promising response, a number that *I* ( and not the other party) suggest. If the party fails to comply with a stated bracket proposal, even a counter-bracket proposal may well indicate where a settlement will lie between those numbers. But not always. Shockingly, I once had in attendance an experienced insurance claims manager who agreed to certain bracket numbers, then convinced me at the end of the day that she had nowhere near the settlement authority that the earlier midpoint number had telegraphed to the other room. I detest dealing with amateurs!

Ultimately in a mediation, very few cases have a chance to settle unless the math works. In both rooms. Experts in negotiation have described this as finding the B.A.T.N.A., or the Best Alternative to a Negotiated Agreement. In exploring this important principle in the late caucus stage in the plaintiff's room, sometimes I will draw for him and his counsel a rough graph that describes "guesstimates" of the ultimate ranges possible in the defense room, plus or minus a 10 to 15 percent deal-making or "gravy" call to the absent supervisor—the "Wizard of Oz." If these ranges fall short of plaintiff's expectation, I focus on "big picture" net returns possible, factoring in future deposition, expert witness, and court costs needed to get to the courtroom. I further emphasize that the battle may well not end there, with the prospect of the further delays of appeals. I conclude with the invaluable emotional savings of simply ending this ordeal today rather than reliving it again and again before trial. I then encourage plaintiff to discuss this privately with his counsel. At this point, able counsel may make their own economic decision to reduce their contingency fee to help with plaintiff's net return. As a mediator, I never initiate that suggestion, as it can lead to resentment by counsel. Good lawyers make that decision on their own. When presented with the prospect of a particular dollar amount net recovery, one feisty 80-something woman once remarked to me, "Well, that's too much to blow, but too little to buy anything good."

In the defense room, less emotional concerns dominate this net return discussion. There, more bureaucratic obstacles prevail, although the issue of future file costs is certainly something worth exploring. I have been known in that room to sarcastically send that message with comments such as, "and if the case doesn't settle today, I'm sure your lawyer will agree to work for free on this file for the duration."

Sometimes (though rarely) when a defendant refuses to believe that plaintiff will submit to a recommended surgery, I might explore a "use it or lose it" escrow account in addition to the settlement number. For example, the defense escrows the reasonable costs of a surgery that would be added to the settlement only upon proof that plaintiff in fact has undergone the surgery within a short-term deadline.

Creativity cannot be overemphasized as parties resist the final flinch to settlement. Sometimes, the lawyers themselves will take the lead. In one mediation, plaintiff's counsel was concerned about his client's willingness to reject a generous offer and resort to trial. He glanced at his client's date of birth in one of the medical records on their caucus table, and cavalierly (and bravely) suggested that for final guidance she check her horoscope in the newspaper available in the reception room. Sight unseen, it worked like a charm. Plaintiff was a Leo, and her day's horoscope warned: "Legal matters are not favored." He suggested that going to trial was not in her future, and the matter settled. Her counsel's only mistake was to resort to the same tactic in his next mediation. His client then was an obstinate Gemini—and her day's horoscope provided: "Others may try to influence you, but do not trust them."

Another plaintiff's attorney at "crunch time" became increasingly frustrated with a client who would call her fortune teller for advice during the caucuses. There was a final offer on the table for $25,000. While the client's attention was diverted, counsel resorted to dropping a quarter on the carpet and quickly concealing it with his shoe, only to reveal it moments later as a "sign from above" that the number was ordained in the stars and tea leaves. He had successfully appealed to his audience that day.

Sometimes impasse-breaking events occur almost providentially. In a matter I mediated, the parties were at odds as to whether the subject casino elevator had actually malfunctioned by shaking, which plaintiff contended had aggravated his recently operated lumbar spine. After several hours of jousting, grandstanding, and Monopoly numbering, just when the level of frustration and pessimism was near a boiling point, someone in the defense room played yet again a grainy video from a camera that all such establishments install into their elevators. There she was. "She" was a rather well endowed, middle-aged woman standing in a corner of the elevator. And if you focused ever so briefly on a certain part of her anatomy, Newton's laws of physics were clearly bouncing during the brief elevator ride. Soon thereafter, there was another type of movement in the defense room that resulted in settlement of the case.

During the final stages, I may resort to soliciting a secret "final number" from each of the parties, with the understanding that if the numbers match, the case is settled. If the numbers are too close for comfort, the parties would be strongly encouraged to allow me to work just a little bit longer. In contrast, if they are in different universes, they are free to go home.

Sometimes if the parties are unbending, one or the other will actually write the final settlement terms on a proposed settlement document and sign it, much like an offer sheet in a car dealer's showroom. In some cases, this vehicle gives the appearance of an "etched in stone" offer. But other times, the party receiving it may revise the document with her own executed final counteroffer. In either case, the fact that both parties have executed the same document, even with revisions, adds impetus toward a final settlement.

More frequently, I have resorted to the exercise of a "mediator's proposal." I explain to the parties that in the few hours of a mediation it would be arrogant and unfair for me to place an ultimate exact value on what their case is worth—but that in that time, through confidential caucus discussions and my own perceptions, I could present the parties a proposal based on a three-step mathematical process I had developed and that had worked in many prior mediations. If both parties agreed to allow me to engage in that process (which I sometimes describe as my version of the "powerful cipherin'" done by Jethro Bodine of *Beverly Hillbillies* fame), then I would retire for a few minutes and return to each room with the product of my computation. Each room would then have a set deadline after which I would enter their room and each would tell me in confidence whether they could live with that final number in settlement, without being asked to bleed further. If both rooms agreed to the number in privacy, then, *voila*! we would have a settlement. The key to acceptance of the process would be its confidentiality. If one party in confidence agreed to the number, the other party would not know that fact unless they also agreed—so that there was nothing to lose in engaging in the process, since essentially the proposed number would be a non-negotiable "deal or no deal." And how would I arrive at this proposed number? Essentially the three components would be:

1. My informal opinion of what this case might be worth in the pending venue;
2. The differential between the two parties' last formal offers; and
3. A net return necessary for each room. In the defense room, this would involve my projections gleaned during the caucuses of file reserves, defense costs, and other bureaucratic costs. In the plaintiff's room, there would be other "bottom-line" net recovery projections, one of which I might cynically refer to as the "F-150 Factor" (at the end of the day, after all liens and costs and attorney fees

are accounted for, would I have enough to buy my Ford pickup?).

This proposal process almost always necessarily resulted in a very irregular, non-whole number amount, one that either consciously or subconsciously came to be recognized by the parties as a final no-holds-barred attempt to squeeze the turnips dry. It worked an astoundingly high percentage of times.

Perhaps the most cardinal lesson learned in closing to settlement is that sometimes it really isn't about the money. Sometimes it really is a matter not of principal, but of principle. A wise authority once described this final closing process as "getting WOWD." The latter stands for a "Way Out With Dignity," a fire escape that acted as a face-saver at the end of the day. Here are some examples from my own career.

One matter involved the death of a nursing home resident under some very suspicious circumstances. During the mediation, her family shared with me repeatedly about how very much the decedent had enjoyed her friends and the staff there before her demise. The family had also shared with me that she was a lover of nature and the outdoors, and was an avid hiker in her younger years. And that day, in addition to a reasonable sum of money, the family's final settlement included the pledge by the nursing home to plant a small garden around the decedent's favorite shade tree on the premises of the facility, one that would bear a plaque in memory of their beloved mother.

In another very emotional case, the parents of a 16-year-old high school football player were mediating a claim against a waste disposal company whose truck had killed their son in a vehicular collision. After a very long day, the parties were apart by $50,000 in a possible overall settlement that by then was in the high six figures. The company's representative had had it. By then he was fatigued, and started ranting that the parents were just getting greedy, and that he was leaving. Thinking quickly, I proposed the possibility of paying the difference not to the parents directly, but using it as a permanent endowment for a scholarship in memory of the young man given annually to a deserving member of his high school football team who had exhibited the qualities of sportsmanship that this young man had personified. The representative scoffed that the parents would never accept that, since all they wanted was money in their pocket. I convinced him to let me float this bridge to settlement in the other room. When I approached the parents about this possibility, not a dry eye remained in the room. The mother of decedent insisted that preserving his memory was all they had ever wanted. The matter settled, and the company obtained a tax deduction for its charitable gesture.

Perhaps my most infamous experience of the process of getting "WOWD" involved a very stylish plaintiff's attorney, a quite able and hard negotiator. His opposing insurance adjuster seemed to have developed an instant dislike for him beginning with the joint session. As we reached a distance of only $10,000 separating us, he angrily declared that if that (adjective) lawyer with his fancy (same adjective) tie thought he was getting another dollar from him, he was sadly mistaken. I quickly pleaded to commit to me that he would call for at least another 5,000—if I came back into his room with the lawyer's tie as his war trophy. His eyes lit up—he now could get out of the corner he had painted himself into. I then summarily entered plaintiff's counsel's conference room, and again complimented his stunning haberdashery. I then represented to him that although his tie was incredibly tasteful, it probably was not worth one-third of $5,000. I asked him without explanation to take off the tie, hand it to me—and I would return with a final increase by that amount. As he was taking off his tie, he declared, "You tell that (noun) in the other room that he can have my tie, but that I'm leaving this room with my pants on." The call was made. And never again did plaintiff's counsel wear a tie to any of our future mediations together.

Of course, as with any closing technique, sometimes a mediator can get too creative. This also happened to me. The parties were far apart after several hours. In one room was a very prepared and obstinate young plaintiff's lawyer, holding firm at $400,000. In the other room were three experienced insurance defense lawyers, all well known to me, holding at about 200,000. We seemed to be at impasse. A lightbulb lit in my brain. I recently had had a similar case with a well-known and respected plaintiff's attorney who I also considered my friend, someone with realistic opinions forged in decades of trial experience. I had his personal cell number on my contacts list. I proposed that the defendants give me one more shot at a reality check with their young opponent. I asked them to let me propose to him that I would call the elder lawyer and blindly ask him for his opinion of what this case might be worth in Baton Rouge. They were at first quite hesitant, but I convinced them that at this point they had little to lose. They grudgingly agreed. I marched into the plaintiff's room and asked the lawyer if he had ever heard of the lawyer who was my friend. He said he did not know him, but that he certainly had an outstanding reputation. I asked if he minded if I called him, described the facts of the case in his presence, and in the confidentiality of the room asked for his opinion of what the case might be worth. He agreed emphatically. The call was made. I reached my friend, who from the background noise was apparently at a local restaurant. I told him he was on a speaker. I asked for five minutes of his time, and described the essential facts of the case. I turned to plaintiff's lawyer and had him agree that I had made a fair and comprehensive description of the case. I then asked my friend for his opinion of what that case might be worth. Without batting an eyelash, he responded, "Oh, geez, Vince, that's worth at least half a million." Immediately I heard the young lawyer respond with an enthusiastic "*Thank you*, Mr. ____!" It was then my dreaded duty to crawl back to report to the defense room that this mediation, for the time being, was adjourned. Later that night, I could not resist calling back my friend to examine his sanity. His reply? I had called him on a Friday afternoon in the middle of his third glass of an emboldening white wine.

And if despite your herculean efforts the parties fail to settle come mediation day, never ever proclaim that the mediation is terminated. Simply say it is adjourned. More on this topic later.

## Chapter 8

# The Marlin Is Next to the Boat: Grab the Net!

One of my favorite novels is Hemingway's *The Old Man and the Sea.* Most of you have read it. Think of the untold hours of physical sacrifice and dogged determination by that simple fisherman, only to witness his prized marlin, tied to his modest boat, shredded away by a pack of voracious sharks. If only his vessel had been big enough to haul the marlin aboard and protect his catch from the marauders. The same lesson applies to a settlement you have just helped to forge among the parties. Often, with flight schedules or fatigue or other sundry alibis, someone will suggest we all go home and commit the terms to writing in the morning. Padlock the doors!

Even if you simply commit the basic terms to writing and signed by all counsel for all parties, this is well worth the extra few minutes of time and effort. Well, there *was* that time in an intellectual property mediation when the parties agreed at 8:00 p.m., only to negotiate the written terms until 2:00 a.m.—my last intellectual property mediation.

Getting some sort of settlement agreement written and signed on mediation day is essential, for several reasons. First, you do not want any party to develop a case of "morning after blues" that threatens the accord. Second, when a party returns to her office or home, those not invested in the mediation, who were not there to experience the blow-by-blow give and take of the process, can undermine your agreement and convince the party that she was robbed. If even only the barest terms are put into writing and the parties or their lawyers sign it, your accord then becomes legally enforceable and immune from second-guessing, like any other written contract. Several decisions in Louisiana have enforced such mediation agreements. See, for example, *Walk, Haydel v. Coastal Power*, 720 So2d 372 (La. App., 4th Cir., 1998).

Equally important is the necessity to have the parties' lawyers write the terms. Many times, one party or another will ask that you as mediator draft the written agreement. Very bad idea, for several reasons. First, as a mediator you do not want to cross the line to practicing law that day. To do so may impact your insurance coverage. This issue will be further discussed in chapter 10. Second, drafting such a document may well threaten your sacrosanct status as a neutral. Just as importantly, the use of the wrong word or phrase, ambiguously interpreted, may result in your exposure to liability for misrepresenting the facts or extent of a settlement. By all means, keep your pen in your pocket at settlement time.

In the event a matter does not quite settle at mediation and the parties suggest you continue negotiations by phone on some other day, do your best to keep them in their seats and herd them to the finish line that very day. If you let them leave when so close, you risk losing the momentum gained—and the resistance lost—throughout that day. You also may find that follow-up calls go the way of terminal telephone tag, or that follow-up texts or emails lose a lot in translation.

On some occasions when settlement is not achieved, the parties may suggest that, since you are now so knowledgeable of the issues in the case, you act not as a mediator, but as a binding arbitrator in reaching an ultimate number. I have learned through experience that while this sounds like an attractive and logical alternative, it is fraught with professional hazards for a mediator. By its nature, in a mediation you have learned in the privacy of caucus rooms information and insights not available to an arbitrator. Often this includes data that a party would not want you to share with other parties. It is not possible to "un-ring such bells" when transforming into an arbitrator. Just as importantly, by ruling in a case as an arbitrator (as opposed to persuading in a case as a mediator), you are essentially making credibility calls that may well jeopardize future mediation business from a losing party.

Of course, I could not conclude a chapter without at least one true story of what happened one day after we had hammered out an oral mediation agreement. I entitled this story "Just Following Orders" when I wrote about it in a bar journal. Sometimes it is better just not to know. I was the mediator in a matter involving a 70-something-year-old lady who sued an auto repair shop after she tripped over an unmarked speed bump at twilight as she crossed the parking area to retrieve her vehicle. Her fall caused her various bumps and bruises, as well as a compound fracture of her right wrist, which required surgery. On the morning of mediation, the blue-haired matron shuffled up the hallway, escorted by her lawyer. I extended my hand to her, and she offered her left hand for a feeble handshake, telling me, "I can't use my right hand." Off we went into the conference room for our joint session. We passed around the mediation confidentiality agreement for everyone to sign. When it reached her part of the table, her voice shaking ever so slightly, she declared demurely that since she could not use her right hand, she would do her best to sign it with her left. Trembling, she scribbled her name and passed the sheet. In a few hours we had reached a consensus. Defense lawyer and his client prepared the proposed deal in writing, signed off on it and remained ensconced in their own conference room. I brought the document into plaintiff's room. Her lawyer summarily reviewed it, signed it, and passed it to his client for her signature. She eyeballed the agreement, turned to her lawyer, and with a hint of naughtiness in her eyes, she inquired, "*Now* may I use my right hand?"

Signed, sealed, and settled.

Chapter 9

# Truth or Consequences

As a mediator, your license to practice law is irrelevant. The overwhelming authority is that mediating is not considered part of the practice of law. As a result, a mediator is not bound by the ethical canons of practicing lawyers. And no, that does not mean that all ethical bets are off. We are governed by our own specific ethical canons as enunciated in the American Bar Association Model Standards, those of the Society of Professionals in Dispute Resolution (SPIDR), and the Model Standards of Conduct of the American Arbitration Association (AAA). You should review these in detail. Here, we will discuss some of the most prominent rules that have surfaced during my practice.

AAA Section III.(C) provides guidance for recognizing and divulging potential professional conflicts. In chapter 4 I discussed the practicalities of dealing with this issue proactively. The emphasis of your inquiry should focus on any appearance of impropriety. The mere fact that you might have mediated other cases with a lawyer or party in a mediation certainly does not create a conflict. Neither is a friendship with one of the participants, although this issue is a matter of degree. Someone you occasionally see in social gatherings is different from your regular Saturday golf buddy. Prior professional association becomes more problematic.

Previous representation of a party is a "no brainer" that requires disclosure. Prior membership in the same law firm becomes more relevant depending on the closeness of practice association and the amount of time elapsed since the association ceased. As is evident from these examples, there are few bright lines and many gray areas in detecting potential conflicts, and the wise mediator will err on the side of disclosure of any arguably close calls.

Sometimes conflicts can first become evident during a mediation, in the caucuses where information is exchanged. When this occurs, a mediator should first request that the party with a conflict allow your voluntary disclosure of such conflict to opposing parties and then request a waiver. Should he refuse disclosure, then you should seriously consider the awkward alternative of immediately withdrawing based on a previously undisclosed conflict, the specifics of which shall not be divulged.

Another frequent ethical issue is the matter of the confidentiality of the process. AAA Standard V.(D) provides that the parties "may make their own rules with respect to confidentiality, or the accepted practice of an individual mediator ... may dictate a particular set of expectations." In my practice, I made a point in the opening joint session to state to all present that I would assume that anything shared with me could be divulged to the other parties—unless I was specifically instructed not to. Anything that was labeled by a party as confidential would remain as such not only for the duration of the mediation, but indeed forever after.

Sometimes I will share with a party information garnered from another room that is not literal or specific, but rather a gut reaction or "feel" about where the other room is or may go in a mediation. At times, I may describe it as "waddling and quacking like a duck headed for $____." This, in my view, is not an unethical divulging of confidential information. It's simply sharing a between-the-lines perception that a good mediator should be able to glean from prior discussions, dynamics, or nuances in the other room.

On some occasions one party may share with you a development that you deem so crucial to the other room's evaluation of a case that it threatens the entire integrity of the process. One notable example occurred years ago, when in plaintiff's room, during a caucus a call was made to the judge's chambers to check the status of the defendant's pending motion for summary judgment. The motion had just been granted, essentially dismissing plaintiff's case (subject, of course, to post-motion procedures or appeals). Plaintiff's counsel shared this important development with me, and instructed me not to divulge it to the other room, but rather to act quickly to maximize what might be offered by defendants before they also found out about the motion's being granted. His rationale was that he and his client should not be penalized for being more alert as to current developments than had the defense room. After a bit of soul-searching, I took plaintiff's counsel aside and told him I could not ethically proceed on such a basis. I also did my best to remind him that the world is round, and that sooner rather than later, his opposition would obtain the news of the dismissal, and would forever hold it not only against him but also against me for failing to disclose this at mediation. It might even threaten the enforceability of any settlement agreement. I offered to discuss this issue jointly with his client. Ultimately, they agreed to do the right thing and divulge the dismissal to the other room, but arguing that the grounds were appealable, and that the battle was far from over. Fortunately, the case settled later in the day for a discount, but not for a fire sale price. And relationships were preserved.

As a mediator, you will find yourself flirting with maintaining your prescribed role as a neutral during certain parts of a mediation. It may be a position lacking credibility that one room has taken that would threaten your effectiveness if you did not speak out against it in the other room, or perhaps it might be a case where you show empathy with the circumstances of one party or another. Oftentimes you feel like the character "Zelig" in the Woody Allen farcical movie of the same name, pathologically morphing like a human chameleon into a close similarity with those you happen to be with at the time. I submit to you that this is part of your job description as an effective mediator. Granted, it is a challenging tightrope to command without falling into the abyss of partisanship, but it is a necessary part of your salesmanship to be a friend to all and an enemy to none. On some occasions, when in a later caucus, calling upon my past "brownie points," I might advance the position of the other room, someone in the present room may act surprised and ask whose side I'm on. My standard response is that I'm on no one's side—that I can't stand any of them. Hopefully, this produces a therapeutic chuckle.

Other ethical issues may arise at settlement time. One has been previously discussed, involving ill-advised requests that you as mediator draft the settlement terms, threatening both your neutrality and your status as a non-lawyer in a mediation. Another potential problem involves the situation of an overlap in offers. For example, at the end of the day, you know in confidence that defendant can pay $200,000, and you also know the plaintiff will take $190,000. It is indeed tempting in such a case to favor the room that gives you the most business in working for a final settlement number. In my view, this is unethical. A mediation is not a direct marketing tool. When such situations occur, you should strive if at all possible to split the difference at $195,000.

Before leaving the topic of ethics, be ever mindful of your duties as a mediator to the legal system and your community as a whole. Standard IX of the AAA provides that you should strive to "... make mediation accessible to those who elect to use it, providing services at a reduced rate or on a pro bono basis as appropriate." Without sinking into an insufferable lecture of how it takes a village, always be mindful of the valuable skills you have developed that may and should be shared at times with those who cannot afford them.

# Chapter 10

# Taking Care of Business

If you have lasted this far into our own Magical Mystery Mediation Tour and remain determined to give this profession a try, please allow a brief discussion of practical financial matters.

The first of these is the fundamental decision of whether you prefer to enter a solo practice or attempt to be accepted as a panel member of an existing mediation firm. I tried both. Or I should say, I tried to conduct mediations as the only in-house mediator at the mid-size law firm where I was a partner, then opted for joining a panel. My brief experience as a solo mediator convinced me that at least for me, a panel was far preferable. Although as a solo practitioner you enjoy exclusively the income of your endeavors, you would be surprised at the built-in financial and other issues such a practice entails. One elephant in the room is the sad reality that some mediation clients become delinquent in payment of your fees. This inevitably requires you to make the uncomfortable transition from selfless neutral to threatening bill collector. Of course, you can always contract out such services, but this further affects your net recovery.

In contrast, as a member of a panel I found many distinct, tangible advantages. A deadbeat client would be contacted and pursued to the ends of the earth by the mediation company, not by you individually. Marketing efforts such as ads or testimonials to your abilities and skills, which I found both expensive and uncomfortable, were handled by the organization. Infrastructure issues were also significant, including scheduling, providing suitable conference rooms and equipment, and the incessant snacks and drinks and meals (all major food groups) that clients have come to expect. Most important of all was the value of collegiality, the ability at first to be trained and mentored by more experienced neutrals and the chance to bounce around ideas with them or just plain vent about issues that may have arisen. Ultimately, of course, this choice boils down to an individual decision depending on your particular situation and mind-set.

Errors and omissions insurance coverage should also be considered. Typically, coverage for a mediation policy is relatively inexpensive. After all, thankfully there aren't many grounds to file suit against a mediator. The main exposure in most cases is for the costs involved in hiring a lawyer to represent you in matters such as defending against judicial requests to divulge confidential matters that transpired during a mediation. Note, however, that most mediation policies exclude coverage for the practice of law. A practical offshoot of this exclusion, affecting mediators who insist on drafting the parties' settlement agreements, has already been discussed in chapter 8. If you are a member of a panel, generally the mediation group offers you quite affordable coverage through a group policy. In contrast, if you are a practicing attorney and have a mediation practice on the side, a rider for that practice is usually available but can be much more expensive.

Another financial issue is one of the more annoying hazards of the mediation trade—the last-minute cancellation. You have reserved an entire day, in all probability scheduled many weeks or months before, only to be informed at 5:00 p.m. the day before that the parties are not yet ready to mediate. In some cases, you suspect that this occurred because someone failed to review their file until 4:55 p.m.—but, of course, this must go unspoken. I have found that cancellation rates average in the range of 20 to 25 percent of all mediations scheduled. January is a horrible cancellation month. December cancellations are rare, as people want their money and businesses want to close their files before year's end.

A select few mediators have proceeded to charge either a non-refundable scheduling fee or a cancellation fee. Frankly, I have found it hard to reconcile that practice with maintaining a happy client base, especially considering the bureaucratic eccentricities of corporate clients that ignore your individual abilities and instead worry about having to justify such costs to their supervisors. Cancellation fees also place you in the uncomfortable position of choosing who is responsible for the cancellation. By the way, inconsistent application of these fees to different clients is courting disaster. Considering the widely available pool of mediators who do not charge these fees, your best approach from a "big picture" standpoint is to swallow hard and accept the cancellation gracefully as a sacrifice to future business. In the case of serial last-minute cancelers, I prevailed on my mediation group to charge a nominal scheduling fee (applicable as a credit to mediation costs) if the parties wished to reschedule a case that had already been canceled on two prior occasions. No one seemed to object to this arrangement. Tragically, the additional free time from cancellations did nothing to improve my mediocre golf game.

A close cousin of last-minute cancellations is what I refer to as "drive-by" position papers. You would be shocked at the number of accomplished litigators who appear at a mediation and proudly present you and their opponents with volumes of new materials to review just as the mediation is scheduled to commence. One creative trial lawyer had the courtesy to call me late one day before his scheduled mediation set for the following morning. He asked me for my home address, noting that his office would be dropping off a mediation binder to review for the next morning's mediation. My sarcastic reply was that if he would leave it on my doorstep, I would review it in leisure by scented candlelight during that night's bubble bath as I casually sipped on my glass of cabernet. Later that evening I found outside my door a sizable binder wrapped by a rubber band, under which was a single laminated sheet entitled, "Vince's Waterproof Bathtub Mediation Cheatsheet," containing basic facts of the case. I still reviewed his full binder before the following morning, placing sticky notes at crucial spots to verify I actually had examined it. Alas, there were no water spots visible.

Another troubling financial crossroad for a mediator is follow-up time spent in cases that failed to settle at mediation. As stated before, follow-up efforts can make or break your reputation for commitment to a case. The issue is whether to bill for this time. My rule is to wait a bit after a failed mediation before sending a bill. If follow-up contacts result in settlement, then your one bill contains all time spent in mediation, including follow-up time. This avoids client notions of being "nickel-and-dimed." If your post-mediation follow-ups do not help produce a settlement, then you must decide whether the amount of time you spent is worth the business risk of charging for that additional time. If it's a half hour, this should be a no-brainer business decision unless you are as greedy as a downtown pawnbroker. But if the parties were receptive to follow-ups and this results in hours of work, then certainly, as Abe Lincoln noted about his fees as a lawyer, your time is "your stock in trade" and should be billed and paid for, whether or not the matter settled.

As a mediator, you may encounter requests to act as a neutral in other non-mediation areas, including arbitrator, early neutral evaluator, insurance loss umpire, appraiser, or special master. Although these crossover opportunities may seem lucrative and tempting, if your goal is to concentrate on mediations, your best practice is to tread carefully before accepting them, especially from regular mediation clients. Do not be "penny wise and pound foolish." In contrast to mediations, these quasi-magisterial functions in essence require you to make a judgment call or decision, one which is binding upon all the parties. The risk is that even if you do your best to make a fair and correct call, a party adversely affected may hold it against you, forever costing you future bread-and-butter mediation assignments.

And, if you are in this simply for the money, before you invest the time and effort to become a full-time mediator, and with deference to Mark Twain ("There are lies, damned lies—and statistics."), here are a few sobering statistics. There are approximately 1.35 million licensed lawyers in America. Of those, about 11,000 belong to the largest mediation association, the American Bar Association's Section on Dispute Resolution. Of those members, about half (and who knows how many of those are fudging) represent themselves to be full-timers. Fewer than 1,000 report incomes above $200,000 per year. And $1 million annual salaries? Less than 30—or about the same number as starting quarterbacks in the National Football League.

Chapter 11

# Are We Having Fun Yet?

As you can tell by now, I cannot over stress the importance of selective and timely levity in most mediations. I have found that when used correctly, humor acts as a subtle balm that soothes the minds and hearts of many a savage mediation beast. I was fortunate to have an accidental head start on this mediation tool, having authored decades of legal humor columns to the point that lawyers expected me to be funny ("Hi, Vince. Say something funny."). This was both a bonus and a burden. I hope I met that challenge well.

I did my very best to make a typical mediation more fun than perhaps having teeth extracted at your local dentist's office, and used a variety of props and lines to try to make that happen. Once in a while I would purchase a package of fortune cookies and sight unseen would ask a participant to crack one open. Most of the time, we could jointly divine an optimistic message in its ambiguous words. Similarly, there was the aforementioned "Magic 8-Ball" that I might bring into a caucus room. You would shake the black plastic sphere and on its face would magically appear a variety of random fateful messages such as "Go for it" or "Don't stop." Of course, we would all have a good laugh when the message turned out to be not quite as upbeat, such as "Leave now."

I loved that little ball—until someone absconded with it one mediation day. I have my short list of suspects.

Of course, cartoons were my stock in trade, and I can only hope the statute of limitations for my unauthorized use will soon expire. I used hundreds of them as tactful challenges to take overconfident parties down a notch or gentle warnings of counterproductive negotiating styles. Even in grim wrongful death cases I have had occasions in the plaintiff's room to be asked for a timely cartoon. Probably my favorite of all, in its many permutations, was the classic *Peanuts* colloquy wherein Lucy always wore down the ever idealistic Charlie Brown to run and kick that football she was innocently, tantalizingly holding down for him, only to swoop it away yet again. The message that I was a man of my word was always loud and clear—and appreciated.

Gallows comments were also usually well received. I might exit a caucus room with a bad offer, turn around as I was closing the door, and whisper, "Don't wait up for me" or "If I'm not back in an hour, send out the dog sled." Or on my return to a room, I may loosen the tension or build suspense with "Do you see any gaping cuts or bullet holes?"

At times I would encourage "best line" contests between the caucus rooms that hopefully engendered collegiality and cooperation. In one case, involving a vehicular collision with a wayward horse on a highway, I suppose I set the tone in the joint session with my self-description as a neutral "without a horse in this race." Before I knew it, each caucus room was "off to the races." First, the plaintiff's lawyer admonished the defense to "quit horsing around." Before we were "out of the gate," the defense lawyer, questioning the identity of the horse, argued that we were dealing with "a horse of a different color." Later, one room wondered if the other room's suggestion of setting a bracket was a trap—as in "a Trojan horse." It got sillier and worse as the day went on and we grew ever closer to consensus. The defendants wondered if the plaintiff's lawyers had control over their client, e.g., "You can lead a horse to water, but you can't make him drink." In retort, relying on a damaging deposition admission by a defense witness, plaintiff's lawyers quoted language "right out of the horse's mouth." At about this point, I was challenged by someone to produce from my trusty cartoon archives a few worthy equine-themed models. The favorite was an old *Far Side* one featuring a horse missing a leg while tied to a post outside a saloon, with the caption, "The bad side of town." This became a reminder to defendants that their case was not in a favorable venue. After settlement had been agreed upon, when someone mentioned the possible need for a Medicare set-aside, someone noted that this had already been discussed—we were "beating a dead horse."

On another occasion we had self-admitted movie aficionados in both rooms. The resulting best mediation movie line contest that day practically wrote itself:

- Cuba Gooding Jr.—"Show me da money!"
- Jack Nicholson—"You can't handle the truth!"
- Paul Newman—"Who are those guys?"
- Marlon Brando—"I'm gonna make you an offer you can't refuse."
- Roy Scheider—"You're gonna need a bigger boat."
- James Cromwell (in "Babe")—"That'll do, pig. That'll do."
- Vivien Leigh—"I've always relied on the kindness of strangers."
- Clint Eastwood—"Go ahead. Make my day."
- Strother Martin (the warden in "Cool Hand Luke")—"What we've got here is a failure to communicate."

The point of this exercise is at least twofold. First, it helps convey your messages of realistic evaluations without seeming arrogant, ornery, or combative. And just as importantly, a little levity takes mediation participants, if only for a few hours, away from the everyday take-no-prisoners world of legal warfare. And maybe, just maybe, they may look your way again.

# Chapter 12

# Razzle-Dazzle

If you learn nothing else from this book, know this: the most central role you will serve as a mediator is the management of perceptions of all participants in a manner most conducive to reaching a consensus. As the mediator, it is up to you to create, foster, nurture, and fuel the feeling that every party is progressing at least as well as his or her opponent. You must instill the confidence that there is indeed a premium to negotiating all the way to a settlement. You must navigate over, under, and through the omnipresent egos (imagine that!) of lawyers, the fears and anger of injured victims, and the cynicism and insecurities of corporate America. And that's just the beginning.

Your mission in setting the theme for mediation day begins even before the commencement of the opening joint session. Always remember the dictum that "perception is reality" is nowhere more prevalent than in all matters related to a mediation. In keeping with this principle, do not ever—*ever*—accept a car ride with any participant, nor even be anything but friendly and polite with anyone involved in any public places at the mediation site. To cross over into joviality or familiarity will place you at risk of having already-stressed people question your neutrality.

Your behavior should reinforce the fact that you face a single task that day, and that is to help settle that case. Unless your mediation is specifically scheduled by the parties for less than a full day, it is a horrible idea to schedule anything else that places a time ceiling on your efforts. You should mute your cell phone, ignore texts, forget about a March Madness game televised in an adjoining room, and avoid any other activity (unless you are in a locked bathroom stall) that undermines that notion. One novice mediator once inquired whether it would be acceptable to bring her crocheting to a mediation, for the "downtime" between caucuses. There *is* no "downtime" if you are doing your job. If you find yourself alone in the snack room of a mediation office waiting for the next room to summon you, stay standing, and by all means tell the other room why you are standing there like a bump on a log. Better yet, review your notes during this time. Think of what and how you will discuss the issues from the prior caucus, and even think ahead as to the caucus after that. And never eat while you wait unless you explain that you are waiting on the other room to summon you. If you do eat, and they summon you in mid-meal—drop everything and follow them eagerly into their room. You are not being paid that day to savor the red beans and rice with the corn bread on the side.

One veteran mediator often noted that everything you say brings you closer or farther from a settlement. In my experience, I believe that statement deserves a radical expansion. Everything you say, or do, or don't say, or don't do— and when and how you say or do it—can make or break a settlement that day. Tread carefully, but look natural and unfazed in whatever you do or say.

Part of being the maestro of perceptions is your forging a never-say-die attitude of energy and optimism. Ready for one last Yogi-ism? When asked by a reporter if he could explain why he was in a hitting slump, Yogi matter-of-factly responded, "I ain't in no slump. I just ain't hittin' yet."

Framing the other room's positions is crucial in your mediation world of managing perceptions. Once, in my litigation days, I represented a party when the mediator waltzed into our room and nonchalantly proclaimed, "They said they don't believe you're ever going to have your surgery." How much more softly would that lead balloon have landed if he had filtered the argument with a less challenging and more palatable alternative, such as "Please help me in tying down for the other room the date of your planned surgery." Be ever mindful that framing of opposing positions is your best antidote to the cancer of the other room's reactive devaluation. If one room declares it's sunny outside, inevitably the other room will pull out their ponchos and umbrellas. Your job is to tactfully allow them to open the curtains and see for themselves.

Finally, be aware that your job as the ultimate gatekeeper of when, how, or even if messages will be shared between the rooms is not an exact science. It is a learned art. Consider yourself not only the stage manager of this production, but also its producer, director, and choreographer. Now let the show begin!

# Epilogue

# Closing Thoughts: Into the Mystic

---

I was privileged to mediate for over two decades. I grew to believe with deep gratitude that all the experiences of my life had prepared me for this profession of service. Mediating was by far the most challenging, exhausting—and rewarding—activity I ever encountered as a lawyer. On occasion, it even felt like how I imagined hitting that one-iron golf club dreaded by all duffers must feel.

Growing up, I was an addicted baseball fan. One of my heroes was Hall of Famer Jim "Catfish" Hunter, a cool and calm mustachioed farm boy from North Carolina who confounded batters with his dazzling array of pitches. Once, after a rare loss, he mused:

> The sun don't shine on the same dog's ass all the time.

Rudyard Kipling, perhaps in more formal fashion, in his immortal poem "If," wrote a similar sentiment:

> If you can meet
> With Triumph and Disaster
> And treat those two impostors the same ...

So what does all this mean? From my experience, of every 100 cases mediated, probably 60 percent would settle even with a carrier pigeon. Another 10 percent or so were doomed to impasse no matter the skills of any mediator alive. But it is in that other 30 percent, that gray area of fertility and possibility between Triumph and Disaster, where the lessons shared in this book can make a difference.

And if you do get to do this on a regular basis, don't ever delude yourself into thinking that you are the perfect mediator for all parties on all occasions. No such creature exists. Do what you can, and learn something from every single case. The rest is out of your hands.